STARS OF THE STARS

*A Fresh Look at Astrology
with Our Favorite Celebrities*

By Kelli Fox and Elaine Sosa

ASTROLOGY.NET BOOKS • SAN FRANCISCO

Astrology.net Books

San Francisco, CA 94115

©1999 by Astrology.net Books

Library of Congress Catalog Card Number: 99-60522

International Standard Book Number: 1-893933-00-8

Book and Jacket Design by Albertson Design, SF

To David...may he surf into the sunset.

Kelli Fox

To my heroes, M.S. and C.K. Will they ever be equalled?
And to Fen, who reminded me to breathe.

Elaine Sosa

Acknowledgements

Yes, the stars were with us while we wrote this book, but so were many others. Our editor, Krista Bruun, reminded us to keep it simple yet smart. Her keen eye and cyberpencil are in evidence throughout the book. Designer David Albertson saw right into us (with no help from the stars) and gave the book the look we wanted. Thanks also to David and Fei Cochrane of Cosmic Patterns for creating such great astrological software. Lastly, huge thanks to David Fox, co-founder of Astrology.net, for making the book happen in the first place. His willingness to let us play in the heavens makes our work heaven on Earth.

Preface

An individual's astrological, or birth, chart is as unique to them as, say, their fingerprint. It's a snapshot of where the planets were at the precise moment of their birth. Combining the astrological chart with the art and science of Astrology allows us to learn about who we are and to learn more about those we love.

Stars of the Stars offers a collection of charts as a way for us to better grasp the concepts of Astrology. The fact that we use celebrities as our subjects makes the learning process that much more fun! However, the learning shouldn't stop there: with this book, Astrology.net offers you the opportunity to order your own chart AT A SUBSTANTIAL DISCOUNT. Visit us online at http://astrology.net/bookoffer or simply clip out the coupon at the back of the book and send away for your discounted chart. You'll need your birth date, birthplace, and exact time of birth (look it up on your birth certificate) in order to request your chart. We also offer non-birth time charts. If you'd like to know more about your friends and loved ones, order their charts, too. (Think about it, your Moon could be in Sagittarius, just like Oprah! Inquiring minds need to know.)

At Astrology.net, the Web's leading Astrology site, we are committed to educating people about Astrology. Using Astrology as a guide to better relationships and better living is how we see it. That this voyage of discovery should also be fun almost goes without saying! We hope you'll visit us on the Web soon.

Contents

Why The Stars of the Stars?

"What's your Sign?" Ahhh, were it all so simple. For many folks, Astrology is all about their Sun Sign — if it's Taurus, they're stubborn, and their Virgo spouse is obviously a critic. While a person's Sun Sign does speak to who they are, there are many other planets in the heavens, and their placement within a particular Sign greatly influences our being. In other words, considering the entire astrological plan, or chart, of an individual is the best way to get a sense of who they are. That's the essence of Astrology: *a guide to who we are*.

Now we could simply write another book about Sun Signs and Mars and Venus and the angles they all form in the heavens, and then you'd have a whole lot of information — but would you get it? Maybe. There are a lot of ins and outs to Astrology if you want to get it right. For that reason, the easiest way to help you learn it may be to get away from theory and into practice. Within this book, we'll give you the information you need in order to understand how the planets influence us, but we'll do that by using real people as examples. We've chosen celebrities to make our case because most of us feel we know them to some extent. It's easiest to bring Astrology to life, and to learn from it, if we can talk about it in the context of people we know.

Each chapter in this book begins with a summary of one of the twelve Sun Signs. Following each summary are four celebrity astrological profiles, or chart readings. Aries features celebrities born under an Aries Sun, the same for Taurus, and so on. Within each profile is a detailed reading of the placement of the planets in the celebrity's chart, the ruling Houses for these planets, aspects being made between planets, and other configurations of note. While the glossary in this book is your best reference for understanding the terms presented, we'll give you a quick overview below.

Let's start with the **Zodiac**, a heavenly band broken down into the twelve **Signs** as we know them. Each Sign is made up of thirty degrees of longitude and has a number of human traits ascribed to it. As the planets travel through the heavens, they "stop in" at each Sign. Looking at where these planets were at the exact moment of our birth helps us learn more about ourselves.

The **Planets** are a primary focus of Astrology. We begin with the **Sun** which represents the ego, self, and one's identity. It also speaks to the Father and male influences in one's life. The **Moon** is Mother and woman, the nurturer of the Zodiac. It also rules the emotions, memory, ancestry, and the individual's emotional response to things. The **Ascendant**, or **Rising Sign**, refers to the Sign which is present over the eastern horizon at the precise moment of one's birth. It is an indicator of one's persona and the picture we give to the world. **Mercury** is the planet which rules communication, intellect, and the conscious mind. **Venus** is all about love, romance, and a beautiful state. This planet also speaks to sociability and harmony. **Mars** focuses on action, passion, and drive. One's force, both physical and sexual, is also under Mars's domain. Lucky **Jupiter** speaks to just that, luck, while also influencing philosophy, religion, and ethics. **Saturn** takes a harder turn, toward discipline, responsibility, and authority. **Uranus** rules erratic behavior, anything different, and rebellion in general. **Neptune** plays with music, fashion, and glamour while also indulging dreams, illusion, and the abstract. **Pluto**, at the outer edge of the heavens, is all-powerful and addresses transformation, destruction, and rebirth with its sheer intensity.

There are twelve **Houses** in the heavens with each representing a particular area of our lives. If you were to see the skies in the shape of a pie and slice twelve equal pieces, you'd be dishing up the Houses. Each planet, including the Sun and Moon, can fall into any one of the twelve Houses (depending on the time of the individual's birth) and is influenced by that House. The **First House** is the House of Self and speaks to our personality. The **Second House** is the House of Possessions and deals with our material assets and our values. The **Third House**, the House of Communication, is all about expression, intellect, and connections among siblings and neighbors. The **Fourth House**, the House of Home, is about home life and heritage. The **Fifth House** is the House of Pleasure and dabbles in romance, creativity, and anything dramatic. The **Sixth House**, the House of Health, is concerned with keeping us whole while also focusing on our job and daily responsibilities. The **Seventh House**, the House of Partnership, is about marriage and anything to do with playing fair (think contracts or their flip side, lawsuits). The **Eighth House** is the House of Sex and deals with sexuality along with inheritances, taxes, and death. The **Ninth House**, the House of Philosophy, taps into our quest for religion, travel, and higher learning. The **Tenth House**, the House of Social Status, represents career and ambition. The **Eleventh House** is the House of Friends and rules friendship, organizations, and philanthropy. The **Twelfth House**, the House of the Unconscious, deals with the unknown, intuition, and dreams.

Aspects, which are the angular distance (as measured in degrees) between Signs and planets of the Zodiac, also warrant mention in that they address both opportunities and challenges. **Conjunctions** are present when two or more planets are right next to each other in the heavens. This favorable aspect brings out the best energies of each planet. A **trine** is an arc of 120 degrees and is the most favorable planetary aspect. Planets trining each other speak to good fortune with a minimum of effort. An arc of 60 degrees is known as a **sextile** and is also favorable in nature. This aspect denotes opportunity. Conversely, a **square**, an arc of 90 degrees, represents friction between two planets. This results in stress and creates obstacles to be overcome. A **quincunx**, an arc of 150 degrees, is an uneasy aspect which speaks to lessons to be learned. Finally, an **opposition** is present when two planets are exactly opposite each other, or at an arc of 180 degrees. This aspect represents a tug-of-war between two planets and calls out for balance.

Astrology ascribes certain **Elements** (Fire, Earth, Air, Water) and **Qualities** (Cardinal, Fixed, Mutable) to each Sign. Taking the Elements first, **Fire** Signs, as their name suggests, represent a fiery nature. **Earth** Signs are practical and grounded, while the Element of **Air** brings forth the intellectual and thought process. The Element of **Water** denotes an emotional, sensitive, and intuitive nature. Signs attached to a **Cardinal** Quality are all about initiative, whereas a **Fixed** Quality denotes stubbornness and inflexibility. Lastly, a **Mutable** Quality speaks to fluidity and an easy-going demeanor.

Configurations such as stelliums, T-squares, and Grand Crosses, while less common in the heavens, are nonetheless quite powerful. When in evidence, they will be discussed (and they are also cross-referenced in the glossary).

We believe the celebrity astrological profiles presented in this book will help you put a "face" to Astrology, and there's no denying you'll have fun while you're at it! That's the beauty of the stars of the stars.

— KƐY —
to planetary symbols used in this book

A chart wheel shows the position of the planets (in their corresponding Houses) at the precise moment of one's birth. While the planets are usually presented via a glyph (the planet's actual symbol), we have chosen to use more accessible symbology. Our charts portray the Sun and the Moon as we generally see them. Mercury, the Planet of Communication, is a phone. Cupid stands in for Venus, the Planet of Love, while Mars is represented by a man with sword in hand. Jupiter's Good Fortune is illustrated by a crown whereas Saturn's hard work is driven home by a clock. Uranus's rebellious nature comes to you on a motorcycle while illusory Neptune is a mermaid. Lastly, powerful Pluto is a snake.

Symbol	Planet Name	Significant Characteristics
	SUN	Identity, Ego, Male
	MOON	Emotion, Instinct, Female
	MERCURY	Communication, Consciousness, Dexterity
	VENUS	Romance, Love, Culture, Aesthetics
	MARS	War, Assertion, Passion, Drive
	JUPITER	Luck, Philosophy, Excesses, Travel
	SATURN	Hard Work, Responsibility, Discipline
	URANUS	Rebellion, Individuality, Uniqueness
	NEPTUNE	Illusion, Make-Believe, Fantasy
	PLUTO	Power, Death, Rebirth, Intensity

ARIES

Aries: The Ram

Ah yes, Aries, the Sign of the Ram — or is it Rambo? Face it, these folks are firecrackers, ready to jump into action and stir things up. Hey, life's more fun that way! Well, at least for the Ram, it is. As this is the first Sign of the Zodiac, expect the Arian to be fond of new beginnings, an initiator who is quick to get things going. The Arian is not afraid to take charge, either, as these folks are possessed of a great deal of confidence. They are natural leaders and revel in the role of top dog. Whether it's a familiar path or the road not taken, the Arian will step forcefully and purposefully, sure that they are up to the task. Finishing things off is another question altogether, as Arians are not known for their follow-through. Maybe, it's because they're having too much fun playing the game.

Aries rules the First House, the House of Self and Personality. Can you say self-ish? Well, you could, and you might be right where an Arian is concerned. Those born under this Sign are so self-confident that they sometimes forget they're not the only game in town. That said, it's a quality which can be easily overlooked when you consider that Arians are also dynamic, courageous, and an asset to any team. An Arian will never shy away from a challenge. Far from it, these people are the pioneers of the Zodiac, willing to blaze a trail at every opportunity. The only question is whether they'll blow up in a blaze of glory. Yes, these are fiery folks, but it's also part of their inimitable charm. True to the Cardinal Quality assigned to this Sign, its members are go-getters *par excellence*, living for their latest quest (or is that conquest?).

Any Rams butting their heads against the wall can be thankful for two things:
1. Good horns
2. Mars

Ruled by Mars, the Planet of War, these folks know a thing or two about head-to-head combat. That's not a bad thing, though, as this fighting spirit also makes for someone who is bold, energetic, and daring. Refreshing, indeed! The Arian isn't concerned about what others think, especially when there's so much to be done. Arians lead busy lives, bolting from one adventure to the next. This is also in keeping with their freedom-loving spirit. If you're looking for Suzy or Sam Sedentary, keep looking. The Aries-born are quick-minded, action Jackson-type folks who aren't interested in small talk. They'd much rather be putting their considerable stamina to the test.

Since Aries is associated with the Element of Fire, expect a combustible brand of charm from those born under this Sign. Arians aren't known for slinking into a corner at cocktail parties; no, no. They will make a grand entrance and set the room on fire, singeing a few revelers in the process. It's just that the Ram is so enthusiastic! The Arian-born can barely contain themselves, chomping at the bit for the next great project or adventure. Whether it's work, family, or love, the Arian will approach the matter at hand with great zeal. At times, these people will bite off more than they can chew, something which can get them into trouble. No matter, they'll find a way to bow out (not necessarily gracefully) and move on to the next challenge.

If patience is what you're looking for, don't call an Arian. These people want what they want, and they want it now. However, if you're in a hurry, you know where to look. Rams don't always understand why things take time, or why some things simply can't be. Again, they're lucky to have those sturdy horns, because they keep butting their heads against the wall. Even so, this is definitely the individual you want by your side if a battle is looming ahead. Arian courage is hard to beat, and these folks are absolutely fearless.

Does an Arian ever relax? Well, their brand of relaxation is different than most. Sports are a good outlet for overcharged Rams, but the game of love might prove an even greater tonic. Arians love the chase and will go after their intended with a fervor that is unmatched. Yes, this can be relaxing for the Ram. It's also great fun.

Aries rules the head, face, and brain, which means that these folks are prone to headaches and even the occasional cuts and bruises. Ouch! Hey, when you use your head as a battering ram, what do you expect? With red being the color of Mars and associated with fire, it stands to reason that it's the color of the Ram.

The Aries-born are spunky funsters who will never shy away from a fight. They love the game and play it with energy, courage, and determination. The Ram can lead the charge and inspire others in the process. Light a fire under this person? It's already there!

Mariah Carey
BORN: MARCH 27, 1970 NEW YORK, NEW YORK USA

Out of the mouths of babes — well, what came out in the case of Aries Mariah Carey was a voice that could flatten windmills. This child of mixed-race heritage may have suffered slurs and indignities growing up but sang through it all, thanks in part to her mom's vocal coaching. Singing and writing music throughout high school, Carey headed into the big city (in this case the Big Apple) soon afterward. Living the local-girl-makes-good fairy tale, the songstress's voice caught the attention of Sony Music honcho Tommy Mottola, and the rest is history. Carey's debut album, in 1990, fetched her an armload of Grammys and the unwavering attention of Mottola, who married his *protégé* in (what else?) a fairy-tale wedding in the Summer of 1993. Alas, Prince Charming wasn't so princely after all, and the couple separated after a few short years. Even so, the Cinderella story continues, as the sexy songbird continues to belt her brand of pop in ever-shorter gowns.

Born with her Sun in Aries, Carey is a pistol with a potent pop, and we don't mean music here. This gal is competitive and dynamic and fully intends to get her way. Does the Ram ever retreat? Heck no! Ramming ahead is more like it, and the quicker, the better. Carey is resourceful, decisive, and unafraid to fail, qualities which have served her well in her quest for success. With her Sun conjunct Mercury, the songstress's will to act is further strengthened. Her moves may be moot, however, in that Carey is reluctant to see her own shortcomings. Since her Sun and Mercury are opposite Uranus in the heavens, Carey's life won't always be a breeze. The Sun's opposition to Uranus speaks to a willful woman who can be dictatorial and high strung; Mercury's facing down of Uranus is a sign of inconsistent ideas which tend toward a radical viewpoint. With her Sun trine Neptune, however, a sense of empathy walks in the door and gives this songbird the ability to walk in another man's (fan's?) shoes. It's Neptune which ensures that Carey will be quite intuitive as to what her fans want.

With her Mercury in Aries as well, Carey can breathe fire (okay, not literally) if that's what she wants. Expect the singer to engage in needless debate. Impatient is this little Miss's middle name and along with it come a bunch of hastily conceived ideas. Can she push 'em through anyway? Hey, it's the Ram we're talking about here — bet on it!

Thanks to her Venus in Aries (yes, the Ram loves Mariah!), Ms. Carey will be selfish in love, too. To say that her relationships are self-serving... well, only Tommy knows for sure. What the Ram does know is that love is a contact sport: aggressive and competitive. Our Cinderella wants to win, a quality which may compel her to form impulsive partnerships. Further, this woman can spend money as fast as she earns it, making that castle of hers a pricey proposition. Since Carey's Venus is unaspected in the heavens, the singer is

Why does Mariah Carey expect to get her way?

With her Sun ☀ *and Mercury* ☎
*(both in Aries) opposite the rebel
Uranus* 🏍, *this songbird is willful
and quick to push her ideas. Will
others listen? The plentiful Aries
in Carey's chart says yes. Leo men
will be especially responsive to the
diva's pleas — this kitten will purr
in the Lion's den!*

bound to be disconnected from the bonds of love and may stand alone when it's all said and done.

It's her Mars in Taurus which marks Carey as one who will get to the finish line. Much like the Bull, the singer may start slow but has the grit to make it big. She also yearns to make money and will feel best when materially secure. Since Mars is conjunct Saturn, the Planet of Discipline, here, look for Carey to be well-organized and a hard worker. While Saturn tends to tone down Mars's resolve and questions the purpose of doing things, Carey is still likely to have a plan and a fair dose of ambition (thank the plentiful Arian energy in this chart for the latter). Lastly, angering this lady is a bad idea as she can be vindictive when crossed.

A final look at Carey's chart shows Jupiter in Scorpio. Simply put, the actress will be lucky with other people's money (hello, Sony!) and knows of only one way to do things: her way. With Jupiter opposite Saturn, Carey may waver between expansion (Jupiter) and contraction (Saturn), but all signs point to money, and lots of it, at the end of the day.

Birth time source: not available. As a result, references to the Rising Sign, Moon, and Houses may be omitted from this profile.

Celine Dion
BORN: MARCH 30, 1968 CHARLEMAGNE, QUEBEC, CANADA

"La petite Quebecoise" is how Arian Celine Dion was known as a child. The youngest of four-teen children born to musical parents, the *chanteuse* started singing at the age of five and was singing professionally by her thirteenth birthday. Manager Rene Angelil (now her husband) saw big talent in the lass from Quebec and promoted her aggressively, efforts which paid off handsomely in their native Canada as well as in France. Dion's records have sold in the tens of millions on both sides of the pond, marking her as one of the most successful international singers ever. Learning English in 1989, the songstress turned her focus to the U.S. music market. Movies have been good to Dion, too, and not because she can act — it's soundtracks which are her domain. Scoring her first Grammy for the theme song from "Beauty and the Beast," Dion sang one of the most recognized movie anthems ever, "My Heart Will Go On," from the movie "Titanic." How does one top that titanic hit?

Born with her Sun in Aries, Dion is unafraid to blaze a trail and is possessed of a compet-itive spirit which ensures that she will make her mark. The singer prefers to live in the present and loves to get things going, lots of them. Headstrong as well, the songstress can be impatient if things aren't moving along as quickly as she'd like. Since her Sun is conjunct, or next to, Saturn, Dion's Arian spunk gets the cold shoulder from the Planet of Discipline. The singer may struggle with her self-image and will find the best tonic for this to be hard work.

With her Mercury in Pisces, Dion is an emoter of the first order. Mercury speaks to com-munication while Pisces is all about feelings. Put the two together and you have a woman who communicates her feelings through words, or in this case, music. Many Pisceans are musically-inclined and also share a heightened emotional awareness. Consequently, it's most natural for Dion to put her creative ideas into song. Since Mercury is conjunct Venus, the Planet of Beauty, here, the diva's appearance is always pleasing. Dion's charm and grace are guaranteed, and she'll find it easy to get along with others, including her legion of fans. This lady will also function best when in love, so that marriage to manag-er Angelil is a great match for many reasons. Mercury also finds itself opposite Pluto in Dion's chart, a signal that this woman knows how to get her message to the masses. Yes, that "Titanic" song did reach every corner of the planet! Pluto's influence here will also put Dion in touch with dissenting opinions and better prepare her to deal with naysayers.

Thanks to Venus in Pisces as well, the musical marvel values love above all. No wonder she sings those love songs so well! Romantic love is a theme near and dear to Dion's heart, and while Pisces may make things a bit hazy at times, the singer wouldn't have it any other way. Since Venus is opposite Uranus and Pluto in her chart, Dion's forays into love

Why does Celine Dion value love above all?

Thanks to Venus 🏃 in Pisces, this musical marvel adores romance. A titanic love story? Hey, Venus is also opposite Pluto ♇ here — this is as powerful as it gets! Look for "la petite Quebecoise" to cozy up to newfangled Aquarians, and to learn a thing or two while she's at it.

will certainly be interesting. Venus opposite Uranus pegs the songstress as a lover of exotic types and is uncomfortable when bound by traditional commitments while Venus's opposition to Pluto speaks to overwhelming passion in love and marriage.

It's Mars in Taurus which marks the songstress as a determined woman. The Bull's practical yet determined approach reaps plentiful rewards, and that's exactly what these folks are after: money. Looks like the boffo-selling Dion is already there! Those graced by this placement are usually good in business; after dark, they're sensuous albeit somewhat jealous. Since her Mars is trine Jupiter, the Planet of Good Fortune, look for Dion to be an enthusiastic and motivated individual. With Jupiter on the scene, plentiful luck is also part of the plan.

Looking at Dion's chart a bit further, one sees Jupiter in Leo. Expect the singer to live big and to be exceedingly generous. Since her Jupiter is square Neptune, the Planet of Illusion, Dion may fall victim to get-rich-quick schemes as a result of being too trusting of others. Lastly, with Saturn in Aries, the lady with the platinum pipes is hardest on herself, thinking even her best efforts fall a bit short! Hard to believe from Queen Celine.

Birth time source: not available. As a result, references to the Rising Sign, Moon, and Houses may be omitted from this profile.

David Letterman
BORN: APRIL 12, 1947 9:00 PM INDIANAPOLIS, INDIANA USA

The zany antics started early for the gap-toothed Hoosier with the wacky wit. Arian David Letterman began his telegenic career as a weekend weatherman in his hometown of Indianapolis, only to get booted out of the job for his goofball behavior. Consider it a blessing in disguise, since it got this funnyman out to Los Angeles where he practiced his trade at comedy clubs and on a handful of sitcoms. His big break came at the knee of nighttime TV legend Johnny Carson, who let Letterman do a stint as guest host. This led to his own show, NBC's "Late Night with David Letterman" and its barrage of Top Ten Lists and Stupid Pet Tricks that served to redefine nighttime television. When he didn't get Carson's seat for keeps, Letterman bolted for CBS and the renamed "Late Show," where he continues to serve up a slice of wry to all who can stand to watch. Is there any accounting for taste? Probably not, as Letterman's fans are legion.

Born with his Sun in Aries, Letterman is competitive, dynamic, and blessed with a larger-than-life personality. As the pioneers of the Zodiac, Arians are trendsetters, blazing a trail where others fear to tread. Enter those Stupid Pet Tricks and the gaggle of gags which have made this man famous. While independent and free-wheeling, Arians can also be quick-tempered, domineering, and a bit arrogant, making it a toss-up as to who started the infamous Madonna hissy fit. Aries's glow compels Letterman to rush about and jump from one thing to the next with little concern as to whether he'll complete any of them.

With his Moon in Capricorn, Letterman's combustible Arian energy gets a bit of a lesson. The Sign of the Goat in the realm of emotions marks the talk show host as ambitious, determined to succeed, and willing to do the work involved. It can also make him appear rather disciplined and overwrought, even a bit cold. This is further reinforced by Letterman's Sun and Moon making a square to each other. These planets are challenging one another, and in the process, Letterman is left with inner tensions and minimal satisfaction from his efforts. His self-conscious tendencies will cause strain in his personal relationships, and he won't be able to get away from a penchant for self-criticism.

Since his Rising Sign is in Scorpio, Letterman gets an added dose of intensity. This funnyman will appear to the world as one who is probing, powerful, and magnetic. No wonder he gets those celebs to spill the beans! This is also the Sign of one who is charming, influential, and, yes, sexy. With Jupiter sitting on his Scorpio Ascendant, Letterman is looking to teach others and make his values known. Hence, his nightly "hour of power" to the clamoring masses.

Thanks to his Mercury in Pisces, Letterman is intuitive and knows what to say. The Piscean influence on his Planet of Communication has a way of toning down his more shrill Arian

What's really behind David Letterman's Stupid Pet Tricks?
It's an Aries Sun 🌟 *which marks the comic as a trailblazer, although it's Mercury* ☎ *in Pisces which gives voice to his more impractical ideas. The result? Pet chow.*

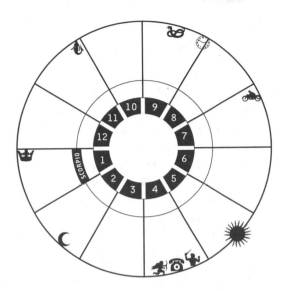

tendencies. Letterman's feelings will tend to overrule his intellect, paving the way for a more imaginative and impractical being. Hence, ideas will be pure play to this man. Letterman's Venus, the Planet of Love, is also in Pisces, making him a bit unrealistic where love is concerned. He'll harbor an illusion of what the perfect romance would be like and would be greatly disillusioned if it turned out differently. This may give way to imaginary romances as an escape from the less-welcoming realities of love. That said, Letterman wants affection and can be tender and sentimental with a lover.

It's Mars in Aries which makes Dave rush into things. The Planet of Assertion is being met by the Ram, so expect a lot of head-butting here. Letterman's approach will be short-tempered and of the "give it to me now!" variety. Since his Mars is in Aries in the first degree (out of 29 possible degrees), one could conclude that Letterman has yet to learn the lessons of this Sign. So if Arians are prone to selfishness, it will be even more pronounced in this case.

Studying Letterman's chart more closely, one sees that his Moon is "out of bounds," an unusual placement in the heavens. As a result, expect a nonconformist. This man will feel how he feels and that's that. Lastly, this chart shows Venus making a square to Uranus, the Planet of Rebellion and Nonconformity. Letterman's pattern will be excitement in his relationships and constant stimulation, especially mental. The fact that he'll be screaming "ME!" at every turn is part of the plan!

Birth time source: Steinbercher

Rosie O'Donnell
BORN: MARCH 21, 1962 COMMACK, NEW YORK USA

It may seem hard to believe, but Arian Rosie O'Donnell wasn't always a barrel of laughs. The funnywoman faced a challenging childhood, losing her mother while still a kid. Television became O'Donnell's companion, as she devoured everything from sitcoms to soaps. With her deft comic touch, O'Donnell worked the club circuit early in her career. The drill paid off when Penny Marshall (a childhood idol) cast the comedienne as Madonna's sidekick in "A League of Their Own." More sidekick roles followed, most notably as Meg Ryan's pal in "Sleepless in Seattle" and as Betty Rubble in "The Flintstones." Abandoning the silver screen for the small screen in 1995 so as to have more time with her kids (this single mom has adopted two), O'Donnell dropped the last name (a la Oprah?) and reinvented herself on her daily gabfest. "Rosie" allows this funny girl to bring the kids to work, a job which includes schmoozing with "sister" Madonna and "boyfriend" Tom Cruise. Such a life!

Born with her Sun in Aries, O'Donnell is pioneering, courageous, and independent. Rest assured that the fire in this Arian gal (it's a Fire Sign, after all) is always put to good use! Expect the combustible comedienne to be competitive and in charge of her own career. O'Donnell probably didn't think twice about her move to daytime TV, sure that she could make it work. Although she may occasionally act before thinking and won't finish everything she attempts, O'Donnell's record of success will be enviable. With her Sun conjunct charming Venus, look for the actress to be *très populaire*, companionable (she's Madonna's bosom buddy, y'know) and socially active (O'Donnell helms her own foundation). This alignment also pegs O'Donnell as a lover of beautiful things, including money.

With her Mercury in Pisces, the comedienne won't always say what she means. She will, however, be keenly concerned about the feelings of others and knows at least one sure-fire way to make people feel better: laughter. The appearance of the Fish here also speaks to intuition and creative (albeit sometimes unrealistic) ideas. Further, O'Donnell may have a hard time ascertaining fantasy from reality. Since Mercury is conjunct Mars, this funnywoman has a lively mind, quick wit and won't shy away from a debate. With this conjunction opposite Pluto, the Planet of Raw Power, O'Donnell may well use words as swords. She gleans opposing views, retreats, plans her strategy, then delivers the *coup de grace*. That this lady's speech might be peppered with expletives as a result of Pluto's presence (almost) goes without saying.

It's her Venus in Aries which marks O'Donnell as somewhat selfish and self-centered, especially in the game of love. The actress will be almost aggressive, and certainly competitive. Simply put, these folks play for keeps and are ardent (that Ram is plenty fiery) in the romance dance. Remember, this lady did get "my Tommy" (Cruise) on her show after all!

Why is Rosie O'Donnell so sure of her instincts?

It's an Aries Sun ☀ *which lights the fire within O'Donnell. She won't think twice about things, secure in the knowledge that she can make them work. When she decides to play, our Rosie will seek out a soulful Sag.*

Thanks to her Mars, the Planet of Passion, in Pisces, the comedienne is an easy-going soul who can be a bit muddled when it counts. She'd much rather go with the flow than force the issue, one reason she's earned the title of "Queen of Nice." Since Mars is opposite Pluto, however, O'Donnell does have some backbone. Her drive is derived from this alignment, and when the going gets tough, she'll bully her way out of things if need be. Since Pluto also speaks to regeneration and rebirth, it's no surprise that O'Donnell successfully redefined herself as a talk show host.

O'Donnell's Jupiter in Aquarius harkens to tolerance on many levels. The actress may well ascribe to a different code of ethics, but she won't impose her standards on anyone. Since Aquarius is at the 29th, or final, degree here, O'Donnell has lessons to learn from her unique style. With Jupiter opposite Uranus, the Planet of Rebellion, Rosie will clearly march to her own beat. She may be a bit out there, but so be it. Look for O'Donnell to be a rabble-rouser and humanitarian rolled into one. Saturn, the Planet of Discipline, also finds itself in Aquarius in O'Donnell's chart. Expect the comedienne to be sanguine about conflicts and to harbor dispassionate views as a result. With Saturn square Neptune, the Planet of Illusion, things will either be by the book or sheer chaos where O'Donnell is concerned. The actress will forever be torn between what she should do and what she wants to do.

Birth time source: not available. As a result, references to the Rising Sign, Moon, and Houses may be omitted from this profile.

Other famous Arians:

Alec Baldwin
Ellen Barkin
Warren Beatty
Eric Clapton
Claire Danes
Robert Downey, Jr.
Aretha Franklin
Andy Garcia
Sarah Michelle Gellar
Sir Elton John
Ashley Judd
Lucy Lawless
Elle Macpherson
Ewan McGregor
Eddie Murphy
Sarah Jessica Parker
Dennis Quaid
Diana Ross
Quentin Tarantino
Emma Thompson

TAURUS

Taurus: The Bull

Rule #1 when inviting a Taurean over to dinner: use Chinet. If those "bull in a china shop" stories are true, well, you wouldn't want to lose any dishes, right? But wait! Taureans are also great lovers of beauty and have a keen sense of the aesthetic. So, set a pretty table and hope for the best. Those born under the Sign of Taurus are the sensualists of the Zodiac, quick to stroke and caress and surround themselves with pleasurable excess. Life is a banquet to the Bull, which is why these folks need to be careful about overindulging.

Taurus rules the Second House, the House of Money and Possessions. These folks can be rather materialistic, enjoying the good things which success brings. Usually, they are successful since Taureans are among the hardest-working people around. That industrious spirit is the Bull's hallmark, and these folks will usually stick with a project to fruition. Reaping the fruits of their labor, Taureans will indulge in a fine meal, a visit to the opera, or a few baubles for their loved one. Why begrudge the Bull a bit of self-indulgence? It will generally have been well-earned.

The Bull is also gentle and good-natured. All of those who think that Taureans are bull-headed are right, too. As this Sign's Fixed Quality would indicate, the Bull can be mighty stubborn. Trying to move these folks from a long-held belief is ridiculous. Let them believe what they want, and take solace in the fact that this stubbornness is what gets Taureans to the finish line more often than not. In any event, arguing with the Bull will only bring out another not-so-attractive quality of theirs, the tendency to argue a point to death. "It's my way or the highway!" the Bull would proclaim while getting ready for battle. Taureans would much rather get back to work, however, so agree to disagree whenever possible, and move on.

The practical Bull is ruled by Venus, the Goddess of Love. This explains the Bull's appreciation for beauty and the finer things in life. Bulls adore a pretty home and a good meal. They especially enjoy these things when in the company of the one they love. At the end of the day, the Bull is a romantic at heart, wooing the object of their affections with music, art, food, and travel. Hey, Venus wouldn't have it any other way, would she? Taureans can also be sentimental and are at their best when they feel secure. For this reason, they tend to be extremely loyal.

Expect the Bull to be:
1. A stick in the mud
2. A heck of a good gardener

The Element associated with Taurus is Earth which makes for some pretty grounded folks. Leave the pie-in-the-sky to someone else, for Taureans prefer a sure thing. The Bull is also patient and practical and functions best when a routine is in place. If a structure isn't there, the Bull will simply create one. While some may find the Bull to be a beast of burden, slow and plodding, you can expect the Bull to get the last laugh. All that hard work pays off! It's the Taureans who will be having champagne and caviar while their adversaries eat crow.

The Bull's nemesis, however, may be the desire to have it all. The Taurean's love of pleasure can put these folks in the position of working increasingly harder so that they can have progressively more of everything. How many BMWs does one need anyway? "A fern green and an orient blue," the Bull would demur. Thankfully, Taureans will usually catch themselves before things get out of hand since they're also innately conservative. While the trappings of success are important to the Bull, so is the bank account. Since Taureans loathe debt, they're disinclined to overspend. That interest in looking sharp, however, won't always translate over to the physical being. Hard workers that they are, Taureans can be notoriously lazy when it comes to exercise. A walk in the park might feel like plenty of activity to the sedentary Bull.

As the symbol of the Bull would suggest, Taureans are often solidly built and possessed of considerable strength. Even so, these folks would much rather spend their time engaging in gentler pursuits such as painting and gardening. Tactile as they are, Taureans are usually quite good at anything created and nurtured by hand. Bulls are also good at nurturing a relationship, since they're hearts-and-flowers types, ready to woo their intended until the prize is theirs. Since Taurus rules the neck and throat, these folks are more prone to sore throats and coughs than others, though they are partial to singing in the shower! Where colors are concerned, the palette most pleasing to the discerning Bull is an earth-toned one, so look for browns and muted greens.

The Taurus-born are solid, dependable folks who will work hard to get to the finish line. Heaven help those who get in their way! The Taurean's successes will pave the way for the material pleasures they so fervently crave. Success sure tastes good to a well-fed Bull.

Cher

BORN: MAY 20, 1946 7:25 AM EL CENTRO, CALIFORNIA USA

She endeavored to make her belly button as fetching as her long black hair, and that's one reason why Taurean Cher sang all the way to the bank. Having Sonny at her side helped, too, at least in the early days. Quick to redefine herself whenever necessary, this daughter of an oft-married (eight times) mom married young herself, proving irresistible to a skinny fellow named Sonny Bono who had lofty ambitions. Crooning pop tunes such as "I've Got You, Babe" and "The Beat Goes On" helped launch the duo's singing and television career, but their reign (and marriage) were short-lived despite Cher's sexy TV garb. No matter. This diva relaunched her career as a sultry songstress and followed that stint with some respectable acting. From the awkward friend in "Silkwood" to the tormented mother in "Mask" and the love-struck woman in "Moonstruck," Cher showed the world that she was someone of substance, even picking up an Oscar along the way. Love, however, has been a greater challenge.

Born with her Sun in Taurus, Cher is persistent, determined, and materialistic. As the sensualists of the Zodiac, Taureans are also tactile and enjoy surrounding themselves with beauty and pleasurable excess. That said, Cher is earthy as well, exhibiting stability, dependability, and loyalty. Taureans are patient and thorough, which helps to explain why Cher has succeeded time and again despite significant odds; this woman refuses to give up! Cher, like most Taureans, can also appear self-indulgent at times and a bit possessive. Lesser qualities known to her are a tendency to be stubborn and argumentative.

With her Moon in Capricorn, this planetary aspect supports many of Cher's Taurean qualities. Since the Moon is the keeper of one's emotions, Cher is most comfortable as a responsible and cautious individual. This woman's successes have not been a trifling matter to her at all. With Capricorn shining down on her, she's had the benefit of a hard-working, economical sensibility to help her along the way. She may have appeared to be the ditz next to Sonny's wicked wit, but you can bet that Cher played along with the full knowledge that this was her ticket to success. With both her Sun and Moon in Earth Signs, Cher is indeed a grounded woman, one who is stable, practical, and good with money. Her emotions are also likely to be controlled, a key ingredient in her quest for success.

Thanks to a Rising Sign of Cancer, Cher presents herself as the emotional, nurturing mother that Cancer represents. Family is important to her, but as this is her Rising Sign, the question exists as to whether this is simply for show. Deep down, Cher is much more likely to be that businesslike, hardworking woman who yearns to be at the top. As her Venus is in Gemini, Cher needs to be matched intellectually where affairs of the heart are concerned lest she get bored. While Sonny knew how to pull her strings, it's likely that

Why is Cher having the last laugh?

Cher's Sun ☀ (Taurus) and Moon ☾ (Capricorn) are both in Earth Signs, telling us she's practical and grounded. No airhead here! This lady's shtick has been honed to perfection.

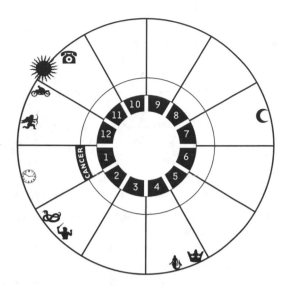

Cher wanted a whole lot more from the relationship. That said, he helped launch her career, which may have been the bargain she sought.

Cher's Mercury, the Planet of Communication, is also in Taurus, making her a slow-talking, well-thought-out woman. Much like the Taurean that she is, she'll exhibit common sense and prudent judgment along with the ability to concentrate when needed. It's her Mars in Leo, however, that can make her a drama queen at times. As Mars speaks to passion, the actress will often find herself leading the charge, exhibiting a willpower and determination which can be quite seductive. When Mars is in Leo, expect a rather robust sex drive, too! It's safe to say that Cher needed her retinue of young lovers to keep her in fighting trim.

Looking a bit deeper at Cher's chart, one sees her Mercury square Mars, a hard celestial aspect. It points to a sarcastic, almost biting individual who won't be topped in a debate. Rest assured that Cher will always have the last word — and she'll always be right. Lastly, this chart shows Cher's Moon and Venus to be out of bounds, meaning that they are outside of the usual latitudes within which planets rest. This positioning is uncommon and can create its own potentials and challenges. Where Cher's Moon is concerned, this signals that her emotions will be a mystery to others. Her Venus, or Love Sign, will also create confusion as others seek to understand her heart.

Birth time source: Lois Rodden

Jack Nicholson

BORN: APRIL 22, 1937 11:00 AM NEPTUNE, NEW JERSEY USA

Those arched eyebrows tell at least half the story with Taurean Jack Nicholson. Ever popular with the ladies, the devilish actor bounced around in B-movies before hitting it big in the 1969 counterculture flick "Easy Rider." Prancing Jack followed this up with his outrageous diner scene in "Five Easy Pieces." It was the role of a zany mental patient in "One Flew Over the Cuckoo's Nest" that finally landed him an Oscar in 1975. Nicholson followed this up with a string of memorable films, among them "Terms of Endearment" (earning another Oscar), "The Witches of Eastwick", and "Prizzi's Honor" with longtime companion Anjelica Huston. "As Good As It Gets," the story of an insufferable obsessive-compulsive, earned the actor his third Academy Award. Gal pal Rebecca Broussard is the mother of two of Nicholson's children, although the actor refuses to play house with this crew. Jack, insufferable?

Born with his Sun in Taurus, Nicholson is persistent, materialistic, and, yes, stubborn as a Bull. The actor likes being in charge and especially likes getting his own way. Taureans are stable and dependable, although they can also be self-indulgent and greedy in their lesser moments. Nicholson's Taurus Sun also happens to be conjunct, or next to, Uranus, the Planet of Rebellion. It's the role of rebel which suits him best – think Easy Rider and that's our Jack! This is a man who is a true original and will try anything once – and he's quite a handful.

Nicholson's Moon is in Virgo in the 29th, or last (anaretic) degree. A Virgoan presence in the sphere of emotions marks the actor as one who is picky, critical, and excessively detailed. He wasn't exactly playing against type in "As Good As It Gets." Nicholson needs to be surrounded by perfection and can't handle things any other way. He may appear a bit cold and detached, but if that's what it takes, that's how it will be. The actor's Moon also contributes to his keen business mind. The fact that Nicholson's Moon is in the last degree of a Sign is a fated placement, meaning that laughing Jack needs to learn the lessons of this Sign. With Virgo, what he has to learn is that he needn't be so critical and that he'd greatly benefit from kicking back and letting some obsessions go. Nicholson's Moon holds more tricks in store: it's making an exact opposition to Saturn. There are three factors to consider here: the Moon is feminine energy, Virgo tends toward a cool aloofness, and Saturn is the taskmaster of the heavens. Put them all together and what you get is someone who sees women as a challenge, whose feelings about the opposite sex are rather skewed, and who must be in control of a relationship. Yowza!

A Rising Sign of Leo enables Nicholson to enchant the world. He will appear glib and larger-than-life and possess a flair for the dramatic. Since Pluto, the Planet of Raw Power, is

Why is Jack Nicholson one of Hollywood's heavyweights?

With Jupiter 👑, the Planet of Luck and Good Fortune, facing down powerful Pluto ♇ (in a direct opposition), smilin' Jack can't help but be on top!

conjunct Nicholson's Leo Ascendant, his powerful persona will be unmistakable to anyone who's looking. If it appears that Jack's looking right through you, he probably is. Remember "The Shining?" With his Mercury in Taurus, Nicholson's Planet of Communication gets more Bullish energy. Here it will manifest itself as slow yet forthright speech and someone who thinks before he speaks.

Thanks to his Venus in Aries, Nicholson will be self-centered and aggressive in affairs of the heart. His lovers will have to keep up lest they be gone, in keeping with his "my way or the highway" attitude toward love. With his Venus at the top of his chart, expect Jack to be a magnet for women. The fact that his Venus is also making a square, or challenging aspect, to Pluto on his Ascendant is further proof of this man's animal magnetism. Venus and Pluto are both charismatic but in their own ways: Venus at the top of his chart lets Nicholson pull women in, while Pluto gives him the sexy edge to get his way once they're there. Ladies, love this man at your own risk! It's Mars in Sagittarius, however, which lets Jack get things done. This placement in his Planet of Passion speaks to drive, assertion, and a need to get to the finish line but quick. Suffice it to say that Nicholson will be ardent yet restless in love — and yes, Sag is the bachelor Sign of the Zodiac!

You've got to hand it to Jack, though — he's got Pluto opposite Jupiter in his chart. With Jupiter, the Planet of Luck and Good Fortune, facing down powerful Pluto, the world is his oyster!

Birth time source: Lois Rodden

Jerry Seinfeld
BORN: APRIL 29, 1954 6:00 AM BROOKLYN, NEW YORK USA

Mixing it up with the Soup Nazi might not be for everyone, but it's right up the alley of that quintessential New Yorker, Taurean Jerry Seinfeld. Poking fun at his East Coast sensibilities quickly landed the stand-up comic on the nighttime talk show circuit. His big moment, however, came when NBC let him at it for thirty minutes each week. Surrounding himself with quirksters Elaine, George, and Kramer, Seinfeld cast himself, sensibly enough, as a Brooklyn-born stand-up comedian. The resulting "Seinfeld" redefined comic television, proving that even a show about nothing could be wildly successful. After a nine-year run, the comic called it a day — but did he say all he had to say? Probably not, since he once again finds himself on stage — when he's not counting the millions he's making from syndication!

Born with his Sun in Taurus, Seinfeld is stubborn, materialistic (yes, those millions are fun!), and conservative. This sensualist may flit from one girlfriend to the next, but he'd much rather have a feathered nest! That said, Taureans can be self-indulgent and prone to possessiveness. With his Sun in the Twelfth House of Illusion, Seinfeld is a very private person who can be secretive and may at times live in his own mind (this House is ruled by Neptune, the Planet of Make-Believe). The intuitive qualities of this placement, however, are the tools of a comic's trade. Seinfeld's Sun is also opposite Saturn in Scorpio. Hence, Saturn, the Planet of Discipline, is grinding at the comedian's hardworking Sun. Add Scorpio's hard edge to the mix and the result is a chilly, ultra-conservative individual who is extremely disciplined with money.

With his Moon in Pisces, the comic actor is highly intuitive and receptive to people. No doubt his comic touch is a result of his keen insight and the Fish's flair for creative imagination. Those influenced by Pisces in their emotional realm are also compassionate, though they tend toward escapism if the mood strikes. Since Seinfeld's Moon is intercepted in the heavens, the comedian has difficulty showing his feelings. This interception creates obstacles to the expression of his emotional blueprint. Since it's the Moon's female energy we're talking about here, expect Seinfeld to have problems connecting with the women in his life. Having his Moon in the Eleventh House of Friends adds an interesting twist to the comic's relationships with women; he'd much rather have friends than lovers! His kinship with "Elaine" may be truer than you'd think. Lastly, with the latitude of his Moon at 0 degrees declination, Seinfeld has a very young Moon. Translation: undeveloped, almost naïve feelings.

It's a Rising Sign in Taurus that makes Seinfeld appear strong and in control. Think of the Bull's stable, dependable nature and this is what you'll see in this man. With his Mercury, the Planet of Communication, in Aries, the comic is blessed with a quick thought process

Why is Jerry Seinfeld such a hot ticket?

Thanks to Mars 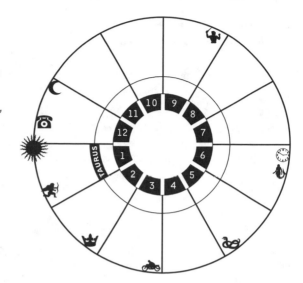 in Capricorn, Seinfeld is driven to succeed in both the bedroom and the boardroom. No bored-room for this man!

and rapid-fire delivery. Can you say comedian? Seinfeld's impulsive speech pattern means he'll say things as quickly as he thinks them up. Since Mercury is in the Twelfth House here, intuition is once again highlighted — the comic can pick up on what's funny without even trying. With Mercury opposite Neptune, the Planet of Illusion, Seinfeld's ideas may be vague and dreamy at times, but Saturn's presence nearby keeps him from going off the deep end with his schtick.

Thanks to Venus in Gemini, Seinfeld continues to be influenced by words. He needs an intellectual match in the game of love or it won't be fun. His part of the bargain will be as a charming, sociable flirt who is loved by all. With Venus in the First House of Self here, Seinfeld comes across as an attractive and companionable lover — qualities which many have seen. Most interesting, though, is the fact that the comic's Venus makes no aspect to any other planet. His Planet of Love is disconnected in the heavens, making Seinfeld's love life untethered on Earth.

Seinfeld's Mars in Capricorn marks him as an ambitious and hardworking man. The Planet of Passion is plenty driven here, especially in the sexual arena, since the comic's Mars resides in the Eighth House of Sex. This fellow is driven to succeed in work and play all the time.

A last look at Seinfeld's chart shows Jupiter, the Planet of Luck and Good Fortune, in the Second House of Possessions. Not only will the comic be rich, he'll be good with his wad, since there's too much earthiness in this chart to do otherwise.

Birth time source: Lois Rodden

Barbra Streisand
BORN: APRIL 24, 1942 5:08 AM BROOKLYN, NEW YORK USA

Taurus Barbra Streisand is a talent for the ages, yet sometimes it's hard to see past her much-ballyhooed features and diva-esque personality. This Brooklyn-born gal started singing and acting early on and was still relatively young when she hit the stage as Fanny Brice in "Funny Girl." The rest, as they say, is history, but it's still a tale worth telling. Streisand has set herself apart by succeeding on many stages. As a singer, The Voice has recorded countless albums and collected an armload of Grammys. Her musical stylings have translated to the small screen as well, where over thirty years' worth of musical specials have yielded numerous Emmys. On the silver screen, Streisand's considerable talents as actress, producer, and director have also been richly rewarded (she has two Oscars). After a series of high-profile love affairs (producer Jon Peters, actor Don Johnson, and newsman Peter Jennings are among her conquests), Streisand has settled into wedded bliss with actor James Brolin.

Born with her Sun in Taurus, Streisand has the Bull's characteristic drive and endurance. Those influenced by this Sign are also reliable and conservative and enjoy a hard day's work. That level of work generally yields the material comforts which the Bull so fervently craves. Expect Streisand to be alternately responsible and unyielding, often patient yet sometimes woefully possessive and jealous. Bottom line: don't look for Streisand to change her tune.

Streisand owes her flair for the dramatic to her Moon in Leo. This placement speaks to one who is self-centered and adores the bouquets and accolades which are accorded a star. Babs loves being the boss but can also be the nurturer, taking great pride in her home and family. Since her Moon is conjunct Pluto, the Planet of Raw Power, here, look for intense emoting from the songstress. Streisand will pick up on the weaknesses of others and use this to seize control. This alignment gets even edgier since it's afflicted by Streisand's Taurus Sun. The diva's Sun is also square Moon and Pluto, creating further tension. The Sun and Moon are very personal planets, so when Pluto is introduced into the mix, things get pretty intense. Simply put, Streisand's Sun and Moon are at war with each other, creating upheaval and allowing the actress to gain little satisfaction from her considerable achievements. A silver lining, however, can be gleaned from Pluto's rebirthing energy: thanks to Streisand's second marriage, the star is reborn!

Thanks to a Rising Sign of Aries, Streisand's image to the world is "all about me." How else do you become a diva? This lady exudes courage and daring and is intent on pushing envelopes. Competitive? Uh-huh, and impatient and energetic to boot. With her Mercury in Taurus, though, Streisand's chatter is well-thought-out. She measures her words and says sensible things which will get her ahead.

Why won't Barbra Streisand change her tune?

The diva's Sun ☀ is square Moon and Pluto ♇ — can you say friction? Mess with her at your own risk. Babs knows she's a star and is intent on keeping the status quo.

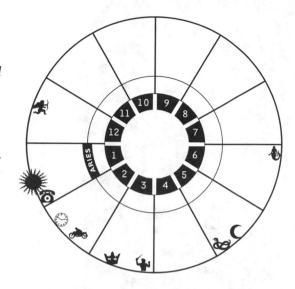

It's Venus in Pisces which defines this lady in the game of love. Streisand has high ideals when it comes to a lover. If her intended doesn't live up to expectations, she'll be disappointed, a common occurrence since her expectations are often unrealistic. Love really rules this funny girl, and impractical as that may be, she's a hopeless romantic.

With Mars in Gemini, Streisand's Planet of Passion gets a real talking-to. It's all about words here, as the actress takes the Twins' penchant for chatter to new levels, arguing at every turn, sometimes simply for the fun of it. Look out world! Or is that colleagues? Streisand's notorious difficulties on the set may get their energy from this placement, as the producer/director's keen intellect can result in a flurry of barbs to anyone in her presence. Since Mars is square Neptune, the Planet of Illusion, here, Streisand's best ideas may be a real stretch. She will talk a good game, but beneath it all will be ill-advised moves and hidden agendas. The actress may also resort to escapism when her seemingly good ideas are given short shrift.

One last look at Streisand's chart shows all her planets except Venus are located below the horizon. This formation in the heavens speaks to a very private person here on Earth. Babs really doesn't want her life exposed — it would hurt her to see a tell-all tome of her innermost secrets. With hubby Brolin, though, she may have found the perfect shield.

Birth time source: Steinbercher, "BC A"

Other Famous Taureans:

Andre Agassi
Candice Bergen
Bono
Pierce Brosnan
Gabriel Byrne
George Clooney
Daniel Day-Lewis
Katharine Hepburn
Janet Jackson
Jessica Lange
Jay Leno
George Lucas
Andie MacDowell
Shirley MacLaine
Al Pacino
Michelle Pfeiffer
Dennis Rodman
Tori Spelling
Uma Thurman
Stevie Wonder

GEMINI

Gemini: The Twins

Blah blah blah. Yadda yadda yadda. This is what it sounds like when there's a Gemini in the room. These folks are the talkers of the Zodiac, and it's not idle chatter, either. The Twins are intellectual folks, the kind of people who enjoy digging around for information and learning a thing or two while they're at it. Their curiosity and quick wit are unrivaled, prompting the less blessed to hurl taunts of "smarty pants!" in their direction. Speaking of school, that calls to mind another quality of the Gemini-born: they manage to seem forever young.

Gemini rules the Third House, the House of Communication. Don't expect to get the best of the Twins in a verbal joust — it ain't gonna happen. The Twins are not only glib, they're also smart as a whip. If you think your argument is solid, they'll go ahead and punch a giant hole in it just for fun. Quick-minded as they are, Geminis aren't likely to stay with one subject for long. Their restless minds will have them jumping from one thing to the next, which calls to question their follow-through. It's true, the Twins may not finish every project they take on, but they're certainly an asset to any team since their quick minds can troubleshoot problems with ease. As a Mutable Sign, the Twins are changeable and somewhat noncommittal. Can you say wishy-washy? Yep, that's them, but it's a label the Twins won't mind. They absolutely love moving from one thing to the next!

Two things you will never get the Twins to do:
1. Sit down
2. Be quiet

Hey, these folks are ruled by the Planet Mercury! Get it? Mercurial. Constant movement, of both mind and body. And mouth. Any Gemini worth their salt is bound to be a big talker, and they are also likely to be well-read on a number of subjects. These people are intellectuals and voracious readers (so what if they read standing up?) and enjoy discoursing on a variety of topics. You might notice that Geminis tend to surround themselves with others of the same ilk. That's because they hate to be bored. Luckily, they won't be boring you, either. Geminis should be invited to any and all cocktail parties since they not only talk a good game but also listen really well. That's because communication for them is a two-way street, a way of imparting knowledge as well as gleaning new information. It's also worth noting that the Twins are loads of fun! These folks are imaginative and clever and always manage to say the right thing. Sometimes they say so much that they can appear to be gossipy.

Since the Element associated with the Twins is Air, naysayers are likely to say "I knew it! They're full of hot air." Come on now, be nice. Air Signs are among the intellectuals of the

Zodiac, putting their hefty brain cells to work on vexing problems and complex projects. If you need a recap of a situation, call a Gemini. These folks don't feel a need to be a leader at work or home, either. Rather, they enjoy working with one or many in order to achieve mutually beneficial goals. Since their attention span can be frightfully short, it stands to reason that the Twins won't complete everything they attempt. That's life!

Energetic as they are, the Twins have a knack for appearing youthful regardless of their age. It's also one of their most endearing qualities. Much like a kid, these folks need constant movement, which makes them a fan of short road trips. Here today, gone tomorrow. That's a Gemini for you, but they'll surely be back, if only to delight you with tales. Geminis love to be amused and loathe routine. For this reason, they may occasionally seem scattered and high-strung. It's easy to overlook this tendency, though, since for the most part, the Twins are affectionate and kind and will win you over with the way in which they glide through life, as if on Air.

When they decide to kick back and relax, Geminis enjoy doing things in pairs. Makes sense: they're a pair already. The Twins are a natural for, you guessed it, doubles tennis. As this Sign rules the hands and arms, get ready for some wicked backhands. Ruling the nervous system as well, Geminis tend to have ants in their pants, something which can lead to exhaustion if they're not careful. When choosing a hue, the Twins should look toward a sunny yellow or sky blue.

The Gemini-born are sterling conversationalists who love to put their considerable brain-power to charming good use. With an insatiable curiosity, they can do three things at once and do them all well. A Gemini sit still? Not!

Johnny Depp
BORN: JUNE 9, 1963 8:44 AM OWENSBORO, KENTUCKY USA

Those with a good memory will recall that Gemini Johnny Depp wasn't always a pouting young man. This small town boy first hit it big as the sexy lad on TV's "21 Jump Street," a teen fest which served up brio and beefcake every week. TV, however, wasn't part of Depp's master plan. The former rock guitarist (he was a member of numerous bands as a youth) switched to films as soon as he could, favoring quirky roles which lent him credibility. Taking on the freakish lead in "Edward Scissorhands" along with the role of patient older brother in "What's Eating Gilbert Grape?" and bizarre director "Ed Wood" helped Depp create a formidable acting resume. Although equally well-known for his off-screen roles (owner of the trendy L.A. club Viper Room, squire to Hollywood glams, and hotel room deconstructor), Depp's favorite role is that of serious actor. Playing opposite Al Pacino in "Donnie Brasco" and taking on the role of gonzo journalist Hunter S. Thompson in "Fear and Loathing in Las Vegas" are further steps in that direction.

Born with his Sun in Gemini, Depp is a talkative and mercurial individual who can do three things at once. Those graced by the Twins can adapt to most any situation and are inventive and quick-witted as well. Since his Sun is trine (120-degree angle) Saturn, Depp is inclined toward serious self-expression most of the time. With his Sun in the Eleventh House of Friends, it's also likely that Depp knows how to make nice. This placement enhances Gemini's penchant for people and making friends, so expect Depp to forge ties with those who can help him reach his goals.

With his Moon in Capricorn, the actor's emotional buzzword is focused. Depp is aloof and controlled, but it's all for a reason: Capricorn's energy signals a plan at hand, and the ambitious actor will enjoy acting on it. Happiness to this man will be linked to his material. Since his Moon is sextiling (a 60-degree angle) Neptune, the Planet of Illusion, Depp's penchant for make-believe gets a dose of positive energy. Read: great placement for an actor.

It's Depp's Rising Sign of Leo which gives him his acting chops. The Lion on the Ascendant marks Depp as dramatic, daring, and courageous. You can just hear him roaring "look at me, world!" No matter, since the picture will be of a bold and self-assured man. The fact that Depp is forever in the headlines with this girl or part of that ruckus is the Lion's doing, too — these folks can't help but attract attention. With his Mercury and Venus both conjunct in Taurus, Winona's ex is a sensualist who is well-thought-out and says what he means in the game of love. While Mercury in Taurus speaks to a pragmatic and sensible (possibly inflexible?) individual, Venus's pairing with the Bull signals lasting friendships and a seriousness about love which can border on possessiveness.

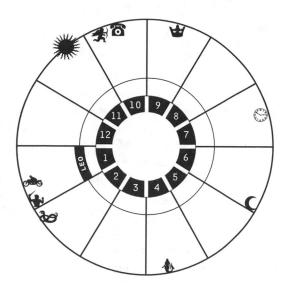

Why is Johnny Depp such a dangerous proposition?

Depp's Mars ♈ is sitting between Uranus ⚷ and Pluto ♇ in the heavens, forming a stellium (the union of three planets). In this case, the resulting energy is aggressive, angry and — look out, world!

Both Depp's Mercury (Communication) and Venus (Love) are square Saturn, the Planet of Discipline and Hard Work, making for some heavy energies. With Mercury square Saturn, the actor won't always speak his mind and finds casual conversation awkward. Venus square Saturn tends to put a damper on affairs of the heart. Depp may be undemonstrative with his mate (which may explain all those broken engagements) and almost perfunctory in love. Further, he has a hard time being happy in love. With Saturn in the Seventh House of Partnership here, Depp yearns for a long-term commitment and takes his relationships seriously, helping to explain the "Winona Forever" tattoo.

Depp's Mars in Virgo is sitting in the middle of Uranus and Pluto, forming a stellium (the union of three or more planets). This placement lends itself to a mean streak which, thankfully, is smoothed over by mannered Virgo. Even so, Depp could easily lose it if, say, the housekeeper messed up his desk! While Mars in Virgo is the Sign of one who is pedantic with details and almost obsessive in nature, this stellium's energy is aggressive, even angry. Mars conjunct Uranus, the Planet of Rebellion, further proves the point: look for Depp to be a daredevil of the first order, someone who craves freedom and excitement at any price. A succession of dangerous liaisons may be this man's version of a relationship. Having Mars conjunct Pluto adds brutal strength and powerful influence into the mix. Bottom line: Depp is magnetic, sexually ready, and willing to use his (physical?) power to win others over. Ladies, beware!

Birth time source: Lois Rodden

Clint Eastwood

BORN: MAY 31, 1930 5:35 PM SAN FRANCISCO, CALIFORNIA USA

Feel lucky, punk? You would if you had the track record of Gemini Clint Eastwood. This rugged *hombre* started his Hollywood career as a bit player but soon realized his chiseled features lent themselves best to cowboy pics. Teaming up with Italian director Sergio Leone, Eastwood went on to make a number of so-called "spaghetti Westerns," playing the poker-faced Man With No Name. Taking the name of Dirty Harry Callahan in the 1970s, the actor starred in a series of shoot-em-up flicks, this time playing a no-nonsense San Francisco cop. Eastwood found time between his various liaisons (which have produced numerous kids) to take the director's chair as well, most notably in the 1992 film "Unforgiven." This Western-with-soul earned the actor Best Director and Best Picture (he also produced the film) Oscars, while garnering a Supporting Actor trophy for co-star Gene Hackman. Eastwood followed this up with "In The Line Of Fire," showing the world that the sixtyish stud can still chase bad guys.

Born with his Sun in Gemini, Eastwood is clever, adaptable, and dual-natured. His quick, dry wit comes as no surprise, since the Twins love to talk and can speak easily on a variety of subjects. While generally congenial, the actor may at times appear restless and eager to move on thanks to Mercury's influence over Gemini. Since Eastwood's Sun is in the Seventh House, don't expect the Man With No Name to be A Man With No Partner. Eastwood needs to be in a relationship and much of his ego will be tied to his partnership. Further, the actor is likely to enjoy activities *à deux* and will work toward a productive marriage.

With his Moon in Leo, look for Eastwood to be generous and warm. Emotionally, this man will have a flair for the dramatic and be especially loving toward his children. Truth be told, apparent tough guy Dirty Harry will have a soft spot for, and take great pride, in home and family. Eastwood's Leo Moon, however, does make an out-of-sign square to Mars in Aries, an indicator that all is not bliss at home. Powerful Mars is in a snit here, so expect Eastwood to get impatient and to take offense at petty remarks. With two Fire Signs (Leo and Aries) lighting up the sky, fireworks·at home may be the order of the day.

It's a Rising Sign of Scorpio which makes our man Harry appear ultra-intense. Ever noticed that Eastwood Stare? Well, it's the Scorpion's doing! The Scorpion's sting on the Ascendant means we see the actor as secretive, fearless, and capable of most anything he undertakes. With his Mercury in Taurus, Eastwood measures his words much like his characters measure their opponents: slowly and carefully. The actor's speech will be sensible and logical, and he'll possess good judgment. Since Mercury is retrograde here (traveling backwards), Eastwood's thoughts and words are slowed down even further. With Mercury in the Seventh House, it's apparent that Eastwood will have difficulty

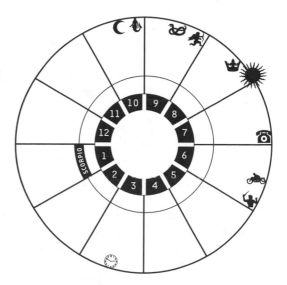

What's behind Clint Eastwood's brooding intensity?

With his Leo ☾ Moon squaring Mars ♆ in Aries, Dirty Harry isn't always Mister Nice. The actor can get fired up in no time flat (and yes, Leo and Aries are both Fire Signs).

communicating in a relationship. Since Mercury is on the Descendant, projection is part of the plan, so expect Eastwood to attract a mate who is just as verbally challenged.

Thanks to Venus in Cancer, Eastwood the family man is once again in full view. Love and marriage go hand-in-hand for our Clint, as do a truckload of kids. The family unit offers a sense of security to Eastwood; since he's good with money, home life should be comfortable. With his Venus opposite stern Saturn, however, the actor may view relationships as a hassle even though he wants one. Sociable Venus just doesn't see eye-to-eye with chilly Saturn, with the result being that Eastwood finds it hard to reach out in love.

Eastwood's Mars, the Planet of Passion, is keeping company with fiery Aries in the heavens. Here on Earth, this placement marks Eastwood as an action Jackson, someone who knows what he wants and will go out and get it. Competitive might well be Clint's middle name since he loves to be in the hunt. Don't expect him to finish everything he starts, however. That said, Mars in Aries is the Sign of a robust sex drive, so we'll hope he finishes that!

One final look at Eastwood's chart shows Neptune, the Planet of Make-Believe, at the top of his chart and conjunct the M.C. Read: this man for all seasons will be well-known for playing roles. The fact that Neptune is trining Mars says there's plenty of "work" to be done and Clint will surely do it.

Birth time source: Lois Rodden

Prince
BORN: JUNE 7, 1958 6:17 PM MINNEAPOLIS, MINNESOTA USA

Prince, aka Prince Rogers Nelson, may have settled for a glyph (in his case the linking of masculine and feminine energies), but to his legion of fans he's simply The Artist Formerly Known as Prince. And quite an artist he is, since this Gemini was a musical prodigy, mastering over twenty instruments (self-taught) by the age of twelve. Helming his own band as a young teen, Prince opted out of high school at age sixteen and stepped into the recording studio. His early recordings, in the late 70s, were both eclectic and controversial yet quickly caught on. Crossing over into pop's mainstream in 1982 with the much-lauded "1999," Prince proceeded to fashion himself a multi-medium career. "Purple Rain," for which he both acted and wrote the score, even won The Artist an Academy Award. The prolific singer/songwriter has titillated fans with recordings such as "Lovesexy" while continuing to write innovative movie music such as that heard in "Batman." Married to Mayte Garcia, one of his dancers, on Valentine's Day, 1996, Prince continues to surprise his fans!

Born with his Sun in Gemini, Prince is curious, expressive, and inventive. As the Sign of the talker, Geminis love the art of communication, and where The Artist is concerned, there is plenty of that in his music. These folks are also versatile, which accounts for Prince's penchant for performing the bulk of the music on his recordings. The singer-songwriter is also a clever fellow, albeit a bit changeable and occasionally lacking in concentration. With his Sun opposite Saturn in the heavens, Prince's general lightness of being takes a bit of a hit. Saturn's influence on his Gemini Sun turns The Artist into a hard worker, one who is disciplined and even self-critical. Since Saturn is in Sagittarius here, Prince will forever be searching for the truth.

It's his Moon in Pisces which gives Prince his dreamy, almost surreal quality. This Piscean Moon marks his emotional state as one filled with sensitivity, compassion, and imagination. The Artist is intuitive and may well prefer a state of unreality to that of the world around him. Since Prince's Moon is at the very bottom of his chart (conjunct the I.C.), it resides in the most personal part of the chart. This placement will compel the musician to keep many of his deepest feelings to himself and to feel torn between the responsibility to his public and his private life. Further, with his Moon opposite Pluto, the Planet of Raw Power, at a hard 180-degree aspect, expect Prince to be extremely intense. This man has strong, almost overwhelming feelings and is a powerful soul. Since Pluto is at the top of his chart (conjunct the M.C.), he is destined for big things and will definitely make a difference.

A Rising Sign of Scorpio is what gives Prince his sexual bent. The Artist's image to the world is of a man immersed in sex and unafraid to talk about what others won't. Think

Why is the Artist Formerly Known as Prince so mysterious?

Since Prince's Moon ☾ *is at the very bottom (and most personal) part of his chart, he is compelled to keep his innermost feelings to himself — and to keep his fans guessing as a result.*

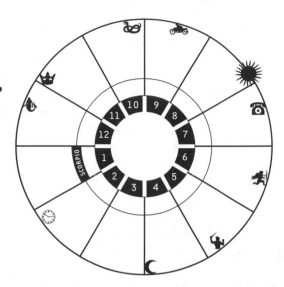

"Darling Nikki," his shocking ode to the real girl world. With Pluto ruling his Ascendant and pulling in some of his Moon's energy, Prince isn't simply posing as an eccentric performer. He really is out there and plenty intent on pushing the envelope. It's The Artist's Mercury in Gemini that gives form to these sensual leanings. With his Planet of Communication visiting the Sign of the talker, Prince is prolific with words and intent on penning as many songs as he can. This man has an overarching need to express himself and is gifted with the kind of perceptive, agile mind which allows him to do so.

Thanks to Venus in Taurus, the man from Minneapolis is a touchy-feely sensualist when it comes to the game of love. Yes, lovesexy is where he's at! Coupling the Bull with the Planet of Love signals dignity, loyalty, and a lasting connection with those that matter. The Artist is also serious and romantic when it comes to love and no doubt intent on making his wife happy. With Mars in Aries, Prince's plentiful wishes are bound to come true. The Planet of Passion is visited by the Ram here, so think energetic action and a desire to get things done. Those graced by Aries in their charts are pioneering, impulsive, and eager — and possessed of a killer sex drive! Looks like The Artist's name should be spelled S-E-X.

One final glance at Prince's chart shows his Sun to be in the Eighth House, the House of (what else?) Sex and Intensity. It's no act: Prince really is as sexual and magnetic as he appears to be.

Birth time source: Lois Rodden

Brooke Shields

BORN: MAY 31, 1965 1:45 PM NEW YORK, NEW YORK USA

Auditions must have started early on for Gemini Brooke Shields. One of her first jobs, as TV's "Ivory Snow" baby, was at the ripe old age of eleven months! You can attribute much of Shields's early success to her mother, Terri, a stage manager *par excellence*. The actress with the ravishing hair and unmistakable eyebrows raised a few (eyebrows, that is) with her performance as a child prostitute in director Louis Malle's "Pretty Baby." Racy ads for Calvin Klein followed, then a sexy swim in the movie "Blue Lagoon." Although Shields's stage and screen credits have been all over the map, she's managed to stay in the public eye thanks to her stunning good looks and a fascination with the question of who this Princeton grad might marry. Tennis pro Andre Agassi provided the answer to the nuptials puzzle. Her TV role as a journalist on "Suddenly Susan" has enabled Shields to redefine herself as a comic actress.

Born with her Sun in Gemini, Shields is a good talker who is versatile and can do many things at once. Those born under this Sign are easily bored, so they need to have a lot going on. Gemini is also the Sign of the flirt, so it comes as no surprise that Shields had those Calvins painted on. These folks know how to catch someone's eye! Expect the congenial Shields to have many friends and to flit with them from one thing to the next. With her Moon in Gemini as well, the ruler of Shields's emotions magnifies many of her Sun Sign qualities. The actress is extremely quick-witted and intellectually inclined, since those graced with a Gemini Moon enjoy poring over books and collecting information any way they can. Conversation is always preferable, though, as these folks live for chatter. At times (suddenly?), "Susan" might find herself restless and in a changeable mood, even lacking follow-through. More often than not, though, the Gemini-aligned make for good pals.

With her Rising Sign in Virgo, things start to fall into place for Ms. Shields. The world will see her as detailed, discerning, and somewhat critical. This penchant for exactness, however, makes it a cinch that the actress is good at learning her lines. While exhibiting patience, she'll also project a fair bit of nervous energy thanks to the combination of Gemini and Virgo in her chart. As both Signs are ruled by Mercury, think mercurial personality, an individual who is an effective communicator while displaying great reasoning ability and a keen awareness of her world. It's Mercury in Taurus, however, which slows things down a bit for this bubbly brunette. Shields's Planet of Communication is dominated by the plodding Bull, so expect her speech to be well-thought-out, logical, and practical.

Shields's Venus, the Planet of Love, has a very prophetic position in the heavens. The actress's Venus is in Gemini and conjunct, or next to, the Moon, with both at the top of her chart. This signals someone who is destined for fame and a public life. It also tells us

Is Brooke Shields more than just a pretty (baby)face?

The appearance of a Grand Cross (four planets or points which form a cross in the heavens) in the actress's chart tells us that she is quite complex and much more than meets the eye.

that she will be perceived as beautiful, much like the Goddess Venus. Gemini's influence here provides charm, appeal, and a deliciously attractive quality as well. Thanks to Mars, the Planet of Passion, in Virgo, Shields tempers some of that loveliness with a desire to be the best. There's no doubt that this lady puts a lot of energy into the little things, even coming into work early to improve a script. With Virgo ruling here, she'll also be neat and clean and almost wholesome in appearance. Like Ivory Snow.

One of the most interesting aspects in Shields's chart is the appearance of a Grand Cross. This aspect consists of four planets or points which form a cross in the heavens: it's also a very challenging aspect. What we glean from this is that while Shields may appear light and easy-going, she is really quite complex. She's had to work very hard to get to where she's at and to overcome many challenges along the way. Don't be fooled by this gal — there's a lot going on underneath! Probing a bit further, one sees that Shields has an unaspected Mercury, meaning that this planet makes no connection to any others. This would lead the actress to feel that no one really understands her complex, intellectual persona. Lastly, Shields has eight mutable planets, those of the changeable, fluid variety. With no planets in the Element of Fire, she clearly needs someone to direct her efforts.

Birth time source: Aspects Magazine, Fall '97, via Brooke Shields biography

Other famous Geminis:

Tim Allen
Naomi Campbell
Drew Carey
Courteney Cox
Michael J. Fox
Morgan Freeman
Anne Heche
Helen Hunt
Nicole Kidman
Juliette Lewis
Sir Paul McCartney
Alanis Morissette
Mike Myers
Liam Neeson
Joan Rivers
Isabella Rossellini
Kristin Scott Thomas
Donald Trump
Mark Wahlberg
Noah Wyle

CANCER

Cancer: The Crab

Cancerians are going to be referred to as crabby, more than once. Why not? It's just like them to retreat into their shell when the going gets rough — or whenever they feel like it. That's because they're moody and emotional. See? It's not name-calling. It makes perfect sense.

As if being assigned the symbol of the Crab weren't enough, Cancerians also need to contend with their considerable emotions. These folks seem to feel more deeply than the rest of us, leading them to laugh easily and sulk for no apparent reason. This instant-response mechanism is also in keeping with the Crab's Cardinal Quality which tells us that these are people who react quickly and are fond of initiating. Equally as powerful as their emotions is the Cancerian's love of home and hearth and the family that's usually in it. Crabs are the nurturers of the Zodiac, providing safety and support for their family as well as a sense of its heritage and traditions. Cancerians eloquently and proudly dispense family history about how Great Uncle Harold was a champion hurdler while Grandma Sue marched for the vote. Sitting around at home surrounded by the clan is what it's all about for the Crab. And some clan it will be, for the Crab is a fertile little critter! Expect those born under this Sign to have lots of kids.

While the Crab is usually gentle and kind, everyone concerned should hope that things stay that way, because when these folks are crossed, boy, look out. Crabs are not above using emotional manipulation to get their way. Remember, too, that Crabs have sharp claws. Anyone picking a fight with them should retreat quickly, lest the Crab draw blood. Keep in mind, though, that Cancerians would much rather spend their time mothering their brood than engaging in tit-for-tat spats. That said, while protective Crabs will forgive the one that crosses them, they will rarely forget.

Comfortable roles for the Crab include:
1. Chef
2. Flag-waver
3. Armchair traveler

Ruled by the Moon, the Great Mother of the heavens, it stands to reason that Crabs are nurturing souls who love their family. Since the Moon also influences the tides, expect an emotional sort who could flood you with tears at any moment. Yes, it can be said that Crabs wear their heart on their sleeve. It's part of the Cancerian's charm, though: a sentimental sensibility which makes for one who is loyal to the core. Those born under this Sign are highly intuitive as well and tend to be greatly influenced by the cycles of the

Moon. Can you say moody? Well, many will, and they'd have a point. Cancerians tend to be up and down, possessing an ebb-and-flow persona which could prove challenging. "Too bad," they'd say, "because that's the way it is!" Much of this moodiness, however, can be traced to the Crab's powerful need to protect those they love. These folks will not sit still while their loved ones are threatened.

The Element associated with Cancer is easy to guess: Water. Yep, the liquid stuff is in plentiful supply for Crabs, contributing to their fluid nature and emotional makeup. It also adds to their sentimentality which can manifest itself as a compunction to collect anything that reminds them of the past. Crabs will need a spacious attic for this very reason. The flip side of keeping all this memorabilia is a tendency to hoard things and to become possessive. This clinginess also inspires thriftiness in the Crab, a quality which may or may not be attractive, depending on where you're standing.

Along with the Crab's need to feel safe and secure is a need to feel complete and loved. Enter food! Delectable dishes are the Crab's best friend, and these folks do love everything about food: preparing it, eating it, and sharing it with family and friends. Hosting a big picnic on the Fourth of July is heaven on earth for the Crab, since these folks are also highly patriotic.

When you're as emotional as the Crab is, sports are a really good idea. What better way to release all that pent-up energy? Crabs prefer team sports (one big, happy family) and enjoy playing near the water. Water polo may have been invented for these crustaceans, not that anyone would want to tread water for that long. In the game of love, the Crab is dutiful and loyal and can even be romantic. Face it, their goal is a partner and plenty of kids! Those Cancer babes should be swaddled in silver and white, the colors of the Moon.

The Cancer-born are empathetic, emotional beings who truly understand another's feelings and feel greatly themselves. They also adore family and are the pocket historians of the clan. When it comes to moods, the Crab has a slew of 'em, so get ready!

Pamela Anderson
BORN: JULY 1, 1967 4:08 AM LADYSMITH, BRITISH COLUMBIA CANADA

She wasn't always that blonde. She wasn't always that buxom, either. Cancerian Pamela Anderson, the ubiquitous Baywatch Babe, started out in life as a small town girl. Fresher hair color and a silicone-enhanced chest landed Anderson some cheesecake Hollywood roles, most notably as the Tool Time girl on the sitcom "Home Improvement." Playboy magazine soon noticed the new bombshell and proceeded to plaster her physique on countless covers. It's the way she fit into her swimsuit and jogged down the beach in the weekly jiggler "Baywatch" which propelled the lady from Ladysmith to superstardom. However, her marriage to wildman rocker Tommy Lee unraveled, leaving the young mother to seek comfort in her familial role.

Born with her Sun in Cancer, Anderson loves her family and is most comfortable in the role of mother. The Baywatch Babe, believe it or not, is domestic, traditional, and sympathetic. Those visited by the Crab can be brooding and emotionally manipulative at times, but more often than not, they'd rather be having fun with the kids. Anderson wants to be a wife and mother most of all and would likely be hurt by press which suggested otherwise.

With her Moon in Aries, the actress's emotional makeup is less than peaceful. Think a fiery, quick-tempered lass who can be headstrong and even hasty. Interestingly enough, Anderson's Sun and Moon are squaring each other in the heavens, a significant occurrence. When the Sun's male energy and Moon's femaleness are out of whack, the result can be strain in earthbound relationships. Consequently, Anderson is projecting this conflicted energy and may be unrealistic about those she loves. Further, with her Moon opposite Mars (a very hard 180 degree aspect), the Planet of War is weighing into her relationships. Everything will be a fight, since the blonde bombshell can be competitive and won't shy away from a showdown. It's important to note that Mars is influencing Anderson's Aries Moon, and in this case, the Moon's own ruler is opposing it. This intense friction only serves to enhance the headstrong energy of Aries. As seen here, the Moon opposite Mars alignment also speaks to impulsive emotions, frightful volatility, and perhaps being at war with one's own femininity (the Moon is female energy, after all). Lastly, Anderson's Moon and Mars are in intercepted Houses, which means that you won't always see her (often scary) energy coming at you. Whew!

Thanks to a Rising Sign of Gemini, Anderson appears flirtatious and will know a little about a lot. The Twins on the ascendant are a sure sign of a chatty individual who is versatile and inclined to entertain many careers. Modeling and acting may only be the beginning for Anderson. It's Mercury, the Planet of Communication, in Cancer which gives Anderson her sweet sensibility. She wants to make nice and will also be gifted with an

Why is role of mother most comfortable for Pamela Anderson?

It's a Cancer Sun ☀ which marks the Baywatch Babe as Suzy Homemaker. Pretty Pam, believe it or not, yearns to be supermom!

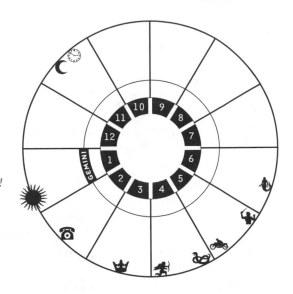

excellent memory, especially of the past. With Mercury squaring Mars, however, a penchant for arguing is introduced into the mix. Yikes!

It's Venus in Leo which helps to make Anderson the vixen she is. Coupling the Lion with the Planet of Love spells drama, romance, and utter attractiveness to the opposite sex. This show pony knows how to strut her stuff! Since Venus is squaring Neptune, the Planet of Illusion, here, Anderson may be a bit unrealistic about love. Is this the Tommy knocker? While Neptune's make-believe energy can be a bonus for an actress, it can spell disaster when choosing a mate. Those blinders are on but good for this babe, and to make things worse, she'll be naïve about money and prone to scams (remember the video?). Poor Pam!

Having her Mars in Libra speaks volumes about our favorite babe. The Planet of Passion is visiting cozy Libra, creating an urge for a satisfying relationship. In this case, however, Mars, which is ruled by Aries, finds itself graced by Libra, its opposite in the heavens. This isn't the most sympathetic of energies, contributing friction to Ms. Anderson's liaisons. This babe will need the approval of others (Mom perhaps?) to help make her relationships work.

Birth time source: Lois Rodden

Tom Cruise
BORN: JULY 3, 1962 12:00 PM SYRACUSE, NEW YORK USA

The road to stardom wasn't an easy one for Cancer Tom Cruise, despite his disarming good looks and megawatt smile. Moved from town to town as a young boy, Cruise turned to sports as a grounding outlet. When a knee injury dashed any hopes of competitive wrestling (really!), he turned to acting. After bouncing around between the stages of New York and L.A., Cruise finally got hot with his winning portrayal of the oversexed teen in "Risky Business." More roles followed, with the action flicks "Top Gun" and "Days of Thunder" paving the way for bigger paydays ahead. As one of Hollywood's most bankable leading men, Cruise has turned heads in films such as "The Color of Money," "Rain Man," and "Jerry Maguire." Married to the comely Australian Nicole Kidman, Cruise stars opposite his actress wife in the Stanley Kubrick thriller "Eyes Wide Shut." Even though he's settling in with his brood, Tom's fans are keeping their eyes wide open.

Born with his Sun in Cancer, Cruise is family-oriented to the core. Those born under this Sign are domestic and devoted. Cruise is a charming mix of sentimentality and good instincts, and you can bet he'll remember birthdays and anniversaries and show up with just the right gift. Lucky Nic! The actor also carries the flag as a true patriot. "Born on the Fourth of July" couldn't have been more right for this leading man. On the flip side of things, Cruise's Cancer Sun casts him as a man who is easily hurt and prone to brooding.

With his Moon in Leo, Hollywood's top gun has a real flair for the dramatic. As the keeper of his emotions, Cruise's Moon pegs him as a larger-than-life guy who is quite at home on the screen. The combination of a Cancer Sun and Leo Moon signals an individual who is not afraid to show his emotions. In general, Cruise is likely to embrace a sunny disposition and feels most at ease around family and close friends. Since the actor's Moon is making a wide opposition to Saturn, the Planet of Hard Work, it's easy to see where he gets his considerable determination. Cruise hasn't been lucky in his career — he's simply outhustled the competition. Although he is warm and loving at home, it's someone else who shows up at the office: a focused, disciplined individual who lives for achievement and success.

Thanks to a Rising Sign of Virgo, Cruise's image to the world is one of a picky perfectionist who analyzes things until he's got them down pat. The actor's clean-cut good looks and perfect smile are also in keeping with the Virgin's penchant for neatness. With his Mercury in Gemini, this leading man is articulate and quick-witted. Expect Cruise to learn his lines quickly and to have a lot to say about a production in general. His agile mind also gives him a desire to learn which is most endearing, so count on Cruise to know a little about a lot. Remember, this man's chart is ruled by Mercury, the ruler of his Virgo Ascendant — and mercurial he is!

What makes Tom Cruise such a top gun in Hollywood?

With Cruise's Moon ☾ making a wide opposition to hardworking Saturn ♄, the actor has been able to outhustle the competition and emerge as a bona fide superstar.

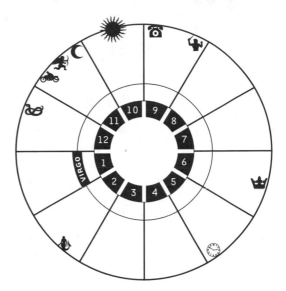

Cruise's Venus in Leo is the real reason why this man is such a chick magnet. The Sign of the Lion with the Planet of Love inspires flowers and chocolates and all things romantic. Cruise is not only ardent in love — he worships his wife! La Kidman is some lucky gal. This lion presence makes Cruise especially attractive to the opposite sex, yet it also brings with it a propensity to take risks. With Mars in Taurus, however, Cruise takes a more measured approach. The Bull in the Planet of Passion is no trifling matter: these folks are patient but determined and driven to succeed for prestige as well as for the material rewards that the big time will bring. Can you say "show me the money?" Cruise certainly can. While his approach may be seen as methodical and slow, his results will always be first-rate.

Looking at Cruise's chart a bit further, one sees Mars square Uranus in Leo. It's this planetary aspect which gives the actor his edge. Look for an action Jackson-type who craves excitement and is willing to push the envelope — both at work and in bed! Yes, his wife is a lucky gal indeed.

Birth time source: Lois Rodden

Harrison Ford

BORN: JULY 13, 1942 11:41 AM CHICAGO, ILLINOIS USA

"The Perils of Pauline" was short one key character: Indiana Jones. Granted, it might have made for a different story line, but as brought to life by Cancerian Harrison Ford, the ever-clever Jones was a combination of swagger, grace, and humility who could tackle any situation. Working as a carpenter between acting gigs, Ford's big break came when director George Lucas cast him in "American Graffiti." Next up was a star turn as Han Solo in Lucas's megahit "Star Wars." The director and his pal Steven Spielberg thought Ford was the embodiment of Indiana Jones, leading to "Raiders of the Lost Ark" and its two sequels. More intelligent, roguish roles followed, in films such as "Blade Runner" and "Witness." No role is too big for Ford as he's even tackled the role of president in the highly-popular "Air Force One." With all this action in his midst, it's no surprise that Ford takes it easy between films at his ranch in Jackson Hole, Wyoming.

Born with his Sun in Cancer, Ford is a strong yet emotional man with plenty of drive. He also possesses the sensitive and instinctive manner which is present in most of his roles. Fluid in his attitudes, the actor can be quite imaginative and is sympathetic to the needs of others. The Crab is gentle and kind and has a nurturing way which can be most endearing. The unassuming Crab can also be easily hurt by ridicule. It can be hard to understand these folks, as their reaction to a situation depends on their mood.

With his Moon in Cancer, too, Ford's Crab-like qualities tend to be magnified, especially where his emotions are concerned. Think of a crab burrowing itself in the sand — that's how these people often feel. Cancerians tend to seek material and emotional security and are loathe to argue unless it's to protect their loved ones. As a rule, those with a Crab Moon are affectionate and loyal and will remember the kindness of others. Since Ford has both his Sun and Moon in the same Sign, the conclusion can be drawn that the actor was more connected to one parent than the other. And yes, family is very important to this Crab-linked man.

Thanks to a Rising Sign of Libra, Indy's alter ego is congenial and sociable and will work hard to keep the peace. No surprise there! Ford will be reluctant to upset those around him, a quality supported by the Cancerian influence in his chart. Libra Rising is also the sign of one who wants a partnership, so these folks usually work well with others. Ford's Mercury is in Cancer as well, and it comes together with his Jupiter, also in Cancer. With the Crab influencing Mercury, Ford's Planet of Communication, expect the actor's intellect to be linked to his emotions. Objectivity won't be Ford's strong suit, and he'll be more inclined to give weight to past events as opposed to the unknown future. Jupiter's contribution here is a tendency to cling to family beliefs, even passing them

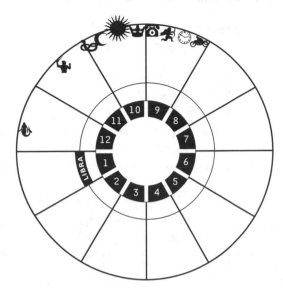

Why is privacy so important to Harrison Ford?

Ford has his Sun ☀, Moon ☾, Mercury ☏, and Jupiter ♛ all in Cancer. Know how the Crab likes to burrow itself in the sand? Well, Ford wants his own castle in the sand, away from prying eyes.

on to children. Home and hearth are also highlighted, and finally, Ford sees himself in the role of teacher, enlightening others through his own experiences, feelings, and gut instinct.

With Ford's Venus in Gemini, it wouldn't be unusual for the actor to talk to his wife all night long. Lucky for both parties, the Gemini influence makes for a great talker, and it's a sure bet that Ford sought out his intellectual match when he said "I do." This placement also speaks to a likable flirt who knows a little about a lot and will engage people at every turn. It's Mars in Leo, however, which gives Ford his more intense quality. The actor's Passion Planet pegs him as a dramatic, occasionally hot-tempered man who is the ruler of his domain. Ford's quest for success stems from this placement, and the issue of success is also a matter of pride for him. The actor's considerable drive also extends to the bedroom, making for a delicious coupling!

Looking at Ford's chart further, one sees that all of his planets are in the top part of his chart, or above the horizon. This is a surefire sign of someone who is destined for public life. Lastly, the actor's Neptune, in Virgo, sits next to his Rising Sign of Libra. This marks the actor as a true chameleon, one who can easily take on varied personae. It's a most auspicious placement for an actor.

Birth time source: Lois Rodden

Courtney Love
BORN: JULY 9, 1964 2:08 PM SAN FRANCISCO, CALIFORNIA USA

The music world did a double-take when it saw Cancerian Courtney Love coming down the pike. No shrinking violet here — Love traveled the world on her grandmother's trust fund before exploring the seamier side of life and supplementing her earnings with the occasional music gig. Her early efforts at pulling together a band came full circle with the formation of Hole, a gritty, punky, in-your-face ensemble. This forum also enabled Love to catch the eye of Nirvana frontman Kurt Cobain, who soon became her husband and the father of her child, Frances Bean. Cobain committed suicide soon thereafter, leaving Love a young widow filled with rage, much of which she poured into Hole's next album, "Live Through This." Love continues to redefine herself without Cobain, alternating between Versace fashion plate and aspiring actress. Not one to disappoint her core fans, Love continues to incite fellow musicians and take the occasional tumble in a mosh pit. What will Love do next?

Born with her Sun in Cancer, Love is intuitive and sensitive yet tenacious when need be. The main quality associated with the Crab, however, is a strong maternal instinct. You can bet that Love holds her daughter close and will nurture and protect her. Cancerians are also helpful and sympathetic and wear their emotions on their sleeve. This feeling sensibility is the Crab's hallmark, although it can at times cause them to become brooding and emotionally manipulative. Ever cautious, the Crab is also keen to call its good memory into service. On the flip side, Love's Cancer Sun is also associated with lazy behavior and a tendency to feel sorry for oneself.

Love also has her Moon in Cancer, which tends to assign many of the Crab's qualities to her emotional makeup. In this case, think of Love as hyper-emotional, no surprise to anyone who has observed the singer. As the Crab is the symbol of motherhood, it makes sense that Love bore a child shortly after marrying. It's also likely that Love will trade strongly on her instincts as opposed to attaching value to hard facts. Further, the placement of both Sun and Moon in Cancer speaks to the likelihood of one parent overshadowing the other.

With her Rising Sign in Libra, Love wants to be seen as a nice person, since the opinions of others do matter to her. She is concerned about her appearance and puts considerable thought into her multiple looks. She also wants to appear connected to another, so it's unlikely that you'll see her alone. Those with Libra Rising know how to charm others when necessary and can call in humor with ease. Enjoying gossip is also part of Love's makeup, though not in a malicious way.

Why is Courtney Love hyper-emotional?

The heavy Cancerian presence in this chart (Sun ☀, Moon ☾) marks Love as brooding, manipulative — and way out there. She'll also trade on her instincts to maximum advantage.

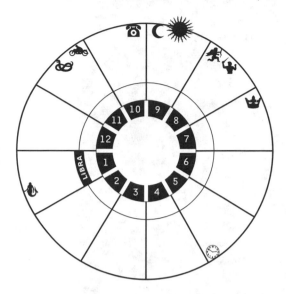

Thanks to both Venus (the Planet of Love) and Mars (the Planet of Passion) in Gemini, Love needs an intellectual match to keep her happy. If her lover can't stimulate her mind, she'll simply move on to the next one. The same can be said of her other relationships: these folks loathe boredom and would much rather flit from one thing to the next until they find the one that feels right. Having her Mercury in Leo simply reinforces Love's spunk. Her Planet of Communication will have her roaring at every turn! Being the big mouth who will exaggerate and say things for effect is what is most satisfying to Love. That said, this placement also yields great storytellers, which may be why Love is such an incisive lyricist. Neptune, the Planet which rules make-believe and illusion, finds itself in Love's First House, the sector of persona and personality, in the singer's chart. This indicates that Love can be very obtuse, making it difficult for others to see the real her. This placement also paints Love as a good actress, so she'd be wise to pursue that goal.

Studying Love's chart further, the heavy Cancerian presence is a signal that this woman was crushed by her young husband's death. It's likely that she would have stayed in the marriage for a very long time. She not only mothers her daughter but probably mothered her late husband as well. Lastly, when Venus and Mars come together as they do in Love's chart, both men and women will be attracted to the individual. Expect Love to be connected yet again.

Birth time source: Steinbercher

Other Famous Cancerians:

Dan Aykroyd
Kevin Bacon
Kathy Bates
Bill Cosby
Anthony Edwards
Danny Glover
Tom Hanks
David Hasselhoff
Anjelica Huston
Michelle Kwan
Frances McDormand
Nancy Reagan
Jimmy Smits
David Spade
Sylvester Stallone
Patrick Stewart
Meryl Streep
Liv Tyler
Prince William
Robin Williams

Leo: The Lion

Madonna. Arnold. Jackie O. It should come as no surprise that Leos are all over Hollywood and just plain famous. They can even get away with one-word names. Now that's clout. As the King or Queen of the Jungle — umm, make that the Zodiac — Leos simply adore their moment in the sun. Since they're ruled by the Sun, they're accustomed to the warm, adoring gazes of their legions of fans. Sounds like a lot of work, but if anyone can handle it, the Lion can. Leos are larger-than-life folks with energy to spare and ambition to burn. With that kind of firepower, expect them to win most of the time. They are also creative and generous of spirit and loads of fun. It's their flair for the dramatic that puts them at center stage a great deal of the time — the bigger the stage the better! That's why so many Lions head for Hollywood.

Since they rule the Fifth House, the House of Pleasure, don't expect Leos to be denying themselves a whole lot. These folks love moonlight and romance and anything that shines a silky-sweet spotlight on them. Those born under this Sign are great lovers of beauty and all things ultra-deluxe. No fixer-uppers for the Lion — that new house had better have gold faucets. "It won't tarnish," this kitten would purr. Anyway, royalty has its standards. Leos are also endowed with great physical strength and considerable stamina, qualities which help them see their projects through to a successful conclusion. This is also in keeping with the Fixed Nature of this Sign. It so happens, however, that Lions are also highly organized, yet another component to their success. Then, there's also the pride factor. Leo's don't know the word "lose".

The Lion is ruled by the Sun, that fiery Star at the center of our universe. This prompts immediate comparisons of Lions as entities who consider themselves to be the center of the universe. Never utter these words in the presence of a Leo, for you'll only upset this dignified cat. Even if they are the center of, okay, let's make that the center of attention, so what? They are worthy of the role. Leos are popular, and even adored, for a number of reasons: they are fun-loving, gregarious, and generous to a fault. Whatever the Lion does, it's done in a big way, since these folks have the self-assuredness it takes to make a statement. Any other reason you'd want to spend your time gloating over this puddycat? Well, Leos are awfully enticing, so they're bound to catch your attention one way or the other!

Tools carried by the Lion's footmen include:
1. A crown
2. A scepter
3. A mirror

Fiery by nature, Leos are also associated with the Element of Fire. These hot tamales believe in acting first and thinking about the consequences later. Hey, this works at least half the time. Lions can charm their way out of any missteps anyway, so this approach is a win-win for this big time cat. While some might find the Lion's approach bordering on arrogance, it must be said that the world will not be won by the meek. And it's the world which the Lion seeks! For this reason, expect to find the Lion front and center most of the time. In the Lion's defense, however, this cat isn't hogging the limelight just for the heck of it. Leos are courageous and bold and truly want to make the world a better place. They just want to be sure that everyone is looking at them while they're at it.

The pleasure principle is one which is paramount in the Lion's life. Weekends in Las Vegas are a particular treat, since the Lion also loves to roll the dice. "Pair of sixes? Hot damn!" And they'll keep on rolling. It's hard to begrudge the Lion their giddy, almost childlike quality at a job well done. These folks love to throw money around and live for a good time. This may make them appear a bit vain and self-centered, but if you were having this much fun, wouldn't you be? When it comes to playing outdoors, Leos prefer group activities. Who will cheer you on if you're jogging by yourself, anyway? Any sport that can be played in a large stadium, preferably with 50,000 seats filled with screaming fans, sounds about right to the Lion.

When it comes to the game of love, the Lion plays for keeps. This cat will zero in on their intended with a laser-like intensity and win. Neither party will complain, either, since the Lion is one of the hottest lovers around. Leo does rule the heart and back, so these sexual athletes need to be reminded that they're people, not pretzels. Satin sheets of purple and gold are sure to envelop the Lion in style.

The Leo-born are creative and courageous and love to win, especially when surrounded by an adoring audience. They are also big-hearted folks whose flair for the dramatic is unequaled. A Lion behind the scenes? RRRRRRRRRRRoar!

Antonio Banderas

BORN: AUGUST 10, 1960 9:00 PM MALAGA, SPAIN

The title of "Latin Lover" is vacant no more with the Hollywood arrival of Leo Antonio Banderas. The silver screen's gain is a bonus for women as the darkly handsome Spaniard is a feast for the fairer set. With his hopes for a pro soccer career dashed early on, Banderas turned to acting and soon landed with the prestigious National Theater of Spain. The eager Banderas next teamed up with Spanish director Pedro Almodovar in a series of films (most notably "Women on the Verge of a Nervous Breakdown" and "Tie Me Up, Tie Me Down") which would establish his movie career. His first U.S. film, "The Mambo Kings," was a true challenge, since the actor spoke no English! Learning his lines phonetically, he turned in a brilliant performance nonetheless. More recent stateside efforts include "Philadelphia," "Evita," and "The Mask of Zorro." Thanks to his American bride, the actress Melanie Griffith, it appears that Banderas plans to stay awhile.

Born with his Sun in Leo, Banderas is dramatic and ambitious and as proud as a Lion. It's a natural that he would have gravitated toward acting, since many Leos take to the stage. Leos are generally fun and creative and can easily command the attention of others. Expect Banderas to be romantic as well, although his image of himself as a hot ticket can cause him to appear vain. That said, his sunny disposition — and, yeah, that sex appeal — will usually win the day. Since the actor's Sun is conjunct Uranus, the Planet of Rebellion, Banderas gets an extra dose of vitality and magnetic charm. Talk about piling it on! Yes, this is a man whose creative energies will be ultra-expressive and quite imaginative. Further, that Leo tendency to say "I'm the boss!" will be magnified by Uranus's presence.

Thanks to his Moon in Aries, Banderas is one hot-blooded *hombre.* With his emotions presided over by the Ram, look for a competitive individual who is headstrong, fiery, and quick to rush into things. Yes, Banderas may be a bit undisciplined when it comes to his feelings, a quality which could get him into trouble in tempestuous Hollywood. Even so, with his Arian Moon in the First House, the House of Self and Persona, it's not likely that this man will hide his bounteous feelings. Banderas's Moon in Aries is also square Saturn, the Planet of Responsibility and Self-Criticism. As a result, he may at times appear distant and somewhat cold.

With a Rising Sign of Pisces, Banderas's picture to the world is that of a lone ranger. Or is that Zorro? This dashing man may appear to be in his own world, a place of wild ideas and untested dreams. The flip side of this Piscean energy is a compassionate and sensitive individual whose liquid eyes speak volumes about his caring nature. Can the sexy Banderas melt those in his midst? You bet. It's Mercury in Leo which will help him keep his

Why is Antonio Banderas such a chick magnet?

A Leo Sun ☀ provides plenty of heat to this Latin lover — and with rebellious Uranus ⛎ right next door, Banderas will not be denied!

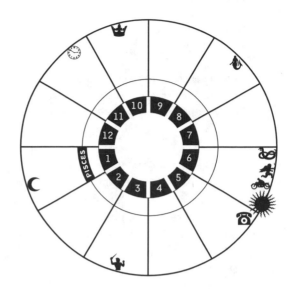

fans happy as this is the mark of a good storyteller. Banderas may be prone to exaggeration as a result of this placement, but he'll certainly be able to entertain.

The actor's Venus in Virgo pegs him as a man of discerning taste. With his Planet of Love ruled by the Virgin, expect a man who is picky and critical where relationships are concerned and even a bit reserved. Banderas is looking for the perfect mate, which in his book may be spelled M-E-L-A-N-I-E. Since Banderas's Venus in Virgo is conjunct (next to) Pluto, the Planet of Raw Power, the actor is a veritable chick magnet who will get whatever, or whomever, he wants. It's Mars in Gemini, however, that allows Banderas to put words to his actions. The actor loves to learn and will debate a subject just for fun. He also craves mental stimulation and will move on to something else if things aren't humming along. The Virgo and Gemini in his chart further serve to give Banderas an ample dose of nervous, mercurial energy.

Taking a closer look at this chart, one sees Venus and Pluto square Mars. Squares in the heavens tend to bring on friction and the ability to get things done. In Banderas's case, the friction is an attraction between the sexes which can be good or bad. When Venus and Pluto come together, it's all about charisma, although their marriage with Mars, the Planet of Passion, may signal a demanding lover who can be insensitive to his partner. Pairing up with this man will be one wild ride!

Birth time source: Lois Rodden

Sandra Bullock
BORN: JULY 26, 1964 ARLINGTON, VIRGINIA USA

The role of girl next door can be a blessing or a burden, but thankfully, Leo Sandra Bullock seems well-equipped to handle it. This daughter of musical and performing parents was exposed to bright lights early on and may have been predisposed to the stage as a result. Heading to New York City in search of fame, Bullock found the road to success paved with hard work. After up-and-down experiences in the theater, the actress moved to L.A., where she struggled some more. Once she commandeered that bus in "Speed," however, Sweet Sandy's days of mixing martinis were over. Her next film, the syrupy romantic comedy "While You Were Sleeping," further cemented the actress's role as the sweet and down-to-earth girl next door. The role of counselor to Matthew McConaughey in "A Time To Kill" served to introduce this leading lady to her favorite Texan (yep, McConaughey). Although the presumed-seaworthy sequel to "Speed" quickly sank at the box office, Bullock rebounded in 1998 with "Hope Floats" and "Practical Magic."

Born with her Sun in Leo, sunny Sandy loves a good drama and is a champion of the underdog. The actress is also idealistic and possessed of a creative and generous spirit. Although the Lion is dignified, those born under this Sign can be vain and pretentious. "But I'm royalty," these kittens will purr, and all might be forgiven. Since Bullock's Leo Sun resides in the first 10 degrees of her Sign, the actress's lionine tendencies are further strengthened. This kitten won't purr – she'll roar!

With her Mercury, the Planet of Communication, in Leo as well, the actress is revved-up mentally. Bullock is a sound thinker who puts a creative spin on things. Although opinionated and even arrogant, Bullock's knack as a storyteller makes it easy for her to be heard. Since her Mercury is opposite staunch Saturn, the actress's tendency toward hyperbole is toned down. Bullock may have gotten in trouble with tall tales as a kid, so she's likely to be much more measured today. With Saturn facing off against Mercury, it's also likely that Bullock's spontaneity will be splashed with a dose of cold water. The result is a more pessimistic outlook on things and a reluctance to embrace new ideas. The flip side of this, however, is Mercury's sextile to Mars. In this alignment, the Speed demon gets a jolt of much-needed energy where conversation is concerned. She will be perceptive and decisive and will state her convictions. Mars's good energy here also speaks to an effective strategist.

Thanks to Venus in Gemini, our gal Sandra is a first-class flirt in the Love Department, a quality supported by her Leo Sun. Expect the actress to be a veritable social butterfly who will flit from one admirer to the next. Those graced by Gemini in the Planet of Love also love to talk, read, learn, and explore. Since her Venus is conjunct (next to) Mars, some of Bullock's explorations may well move into the bedroom! The fact that these two planets

Why is Sandra Bullock a first-class flirt?

With Venus 🏹 *in Gemini, sassy Sandy can talk circles around anyone, all the while batting those pretty eyelashes. Having her Sun* ☀ *in Leo serves to quicken the pace. This Lioness would rather bat it around with a Sag, since the Archer's arrows hit the Bullock bull's-eye dead on.*

are so cozy speaks to sexual appeal and a highly amorous nature. With Gemini in the mix, however, Bullock may be more talk than action. Even so, she'll have plenty of friends with which to play the flirtatious seductress.

Since Mars, the Planet of Passion, is also visited by the Twins, Bullock may find herself arguing just for the fun of it. Our favorite Girl Next Door? You bet. Gemini's energy here can be both competitive and aggressive, so engage Bullock in wordplay at your own risk. The actress is also likely to start many things in keeping with her impetuous bent. And she'll always have the last word.

Looking at Bullock's chart a bit further, we see Jupiter, the Planet of Philosophy, in Taurus. Luck with material possessions is indicated here, as is a practical slant. Further, the actress will need a good reason to believe what she's hearing; she is also prone to overindulgence, a trait reinforced by her Leo Sun. Since Jupiter is opposite Neptune, the Planet of Illusion, Bullock is quite spiritual, although she'll need proof before she backs a new ideology. Lastly, the actress's chart shows Saturn, the Planet of Discipline, in dreamy Pisces, a tough placement. Bullock has dreamer written all over her and desperately wants to believe in that which matters to her most. With Saturn opposite Uranus, the Planet of Rebellion, look for someone who needs freedom and prefers the world on her terms.

Birth time source: not available. As a result, references to the Rising Sign, Moon, and Houses may be omitted from this profile.

Robert De Niro

BORN: AUGUST 17, 1943 3:00 AM BROOKLYN, NEW YORK USA

"You talkin' to me?" So growled Leo Robert De Niro in his memorable role as the combustible cabbie in "Taxi Driver." This seminal role is one of a number of collaborations ("Raging Bull," "Good Fellas") the talented actor has had with director Martin Scorsese, like himself, a graduate of New York City's mean streets. Often playing the strong, not-so-silent type, De Niro's range has been showcased in films such as "Heat," "Casino," and "Godfather II." More at home in the role of father, however, De Niro has five children and a string of high-profile ex-girlfriends. Ask him about any of them and the actor is likely to growl back, since this two-time Oscar winner is notoriously tight-lipped on the question of his personal life.

Born with his Sun in Leo, De Niro is in pretty good company, since there are a lot of Leos in Hollywood. Leo is the Sign of the actor, since these folks tend to be bold, dramatic, and love being the center of attention. The Lion is also popular and generous, which helps to explain why De Niro is held in such high esteem. The fact that those born under this Sign are also attracted to beauty may account for all the pretty women with whom the actor is usually surrounded. De Niro's Leo Sun further speaks to someone who is determined to succeed.

With his Moon in Pisces, one sees even more validation of De Niro's gifts as an actor. Many individuals influenced by this Sign choose to perform or to be creative in some way. Pisces is the chameleon of the Zodiac, which makes slipping from one role to the next a relative breeze for the actor. As the Moon is the director of his emotions, expect De Niro to be a sponge, soaking up the feelings of others. His gift of intuition is unparalleled, making it easy for him to step into another man's shoes.

Thanks to his Rising Sign in Cancer, De Niro's appearance to the world is that of a sensitive and caring individual. The Crab's influence also pegs him as an emotional man, even if he's not quick to show it. Rest assured that things are roiling underneath! The actor, however, is a family man at heart, a role which De Niro takes quite seriously. Cancer's protective qualities explain why De Niro's brood is not out front and center — he would much rather shield those he loves from the glare of bright lights.

With both his Venus and Mercury coming together in Virgo, this good fella is particularly good with details, especially where communication is concerned. De Niro won't miss a beat when speaking with others, yet can be overly critical and picky. He is also possessed of a keen mind. Since Virgo is in the actor's love shack, expect him to be fussy with relationships as well. He is likely to be looking for perfection in his liaisons, which can lead

Is Robert De Niro a carbon copy of the tough-guy characters he favors?

Fiery Jupiter 👑 and potent Pluto ♇ are keeping house with De Niro's Leo Sun. The upshot? An actor who is no lightweight — and can even be a raging bull.

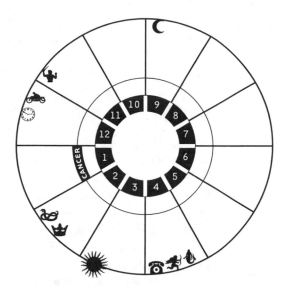

to many an attempt. It's the little things which will annoy De Niro where a partner is concerned, so that tube of toothpaste had better be capped.

De Niro's Mars, or Passion Planet, is in Taurus, which sheds considerable light on the actor's success. This placement speaks to one who is stubborn, materialistic, and fixed in his opinions. That Bull in Mars is a raging bull, a role which this actor knows well! That said, the Taurean influence here tends to inhibit Mars's natural initiative. So, as opposed to racing ahead, De Niro's approach is one which is more purposeful and deliberate. The actor will get to the finish line, but in his own good time. Much the same can be said of this placement's twist on sex: slow and steady. It's also worth noting that De Niro's Sun in Leo and Mars in Taurus give him an edge, sharp corners which mark him as a true contender.

Looking at the actor's chart more closely, one finds Jupiter and Pluto conjunct, or next to each other, in Leo. This meeting of planets is further proof that De Niro is no lightweight. The power wielded by the actor as a result of this alignment is delightfully opportunistic in nature. Give him an inch, and he'll take a mile! Expect the actor to exert his influence over others as well. Lastly, only De Niro's Moon is in the Element of Water, pegging him as someone whose emotions may be a bit stilted. As a result, it's much likelier that he'll lead with his mind as opposed to his heart.

Birth time source: Steinbercher

Madonna
BORN: AUGUST 16, 1958 7:05 AM BAY CITY, MICHIGAN USA

The term "Bundle of Blonde Ambition" no longer applies to Marilyn Monroe now that Leo Madonna Ciccone is on the scene. The former Material Girl and Boy Toy may change her hair color at a dizzying rate, but it all serves to satisfy the media's incredible appetite for the gal from Bay City (Michigan). Using her dancing ability to break into the New York City stage and club scene, Madonna's 1982 release, "Like a Virgin," and its accompanying music videos were proof positive that her cross-currents (religious emblems worn with the shortest of skirts) were here to stay. Eager to conquer the world, this icon-in-the-making made a few movies ("Desperately Seeking Susan" may still be the best), starred in a documentary (the risqué "Truth or Dare"), and even penned a coffee-table text titled, simply, "Sex." After a succession of seemingly incongruous men (Sean Penn, Warren Beatty, John F. Kennedy, Jr.), Madonna opted for motherhood with the help of then-beau Carlos Leon. Daughter Lourdes is an integral part of the mystical (Kabbalah, anyone?) Madonna of the 90s as showcased in the still-danceable "Ray of Light."

Born with her Sun in Leo, Madonna is showy to the max. The Material Girl is a Drama Queen for sure, one possessed of great ambition and keen creative impulses. Status is important to her, and although she fears ridicule, she can adopt the pose of autocrat within her domain. Since her Sun is square Mars, expect the big M to win at all costs. This lady has to be Number One and won't settle for anything less. In this alignment, Leo and Taurus rub each other the wrong way, resulting in the right combination. Mars's passion, coupled with the vitality of the Sun, creates an energy and ambition which cannot be equaled. "Winner" should be the singer's middle name!

With her Moon in Virgo, Madonna's manners are smoothed over. This vixen's emotions will generally be in check, the better to reach her objectives. Virgo's influence in the emotional realm is one of ordered and exacting behavior; those owning this placement are also scrupulous in their work habits and equally fastidious about diet and health. Madonna's Rising Sign, also in Virgo, tells us that she is detailed, neat, and fussy. If she exhibits a steely demeanor, well, this lady also knows how to discipline herself thanks to the Virgin. Lastly, with her Mercury also in Virgo, the actress has the ability to blend logic and detail into one tidy package.

The fact that Madonna's Moon, Ascendant, Mercury, and Pluto are all next to each other in Virgo forms a stellium in the heavens. A Virgoan stellium defines what the singer wants; her Leo energy helps her go out and get it. Pluto's influence here is one of practical action, since the Planet of Raw Power knows how to get things done. Taking this stellium one piece at a time, the conjunction of the Moon and the Ascendant tells us Madonna will

Why does Madonna win at all costs?

Thanks to her Sun 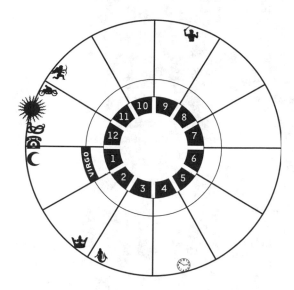 *square mighty Mars* , *Madonna has to be Number One. The friction between these two planets ensures that the actress won't settle for anything less.*

wear her heart on her sleeve. With Mercury nearby, she'll verbalize her feelings, too. The Moon's conjunction to Mercury, the Planet of Communication, signals Madonna's willingness to go with feelings over reason. She'll act on things only if they feel right. Having Pluto close to this alignment gives strength to Madonna's intuition and sensitivity. The Moon conjunct Pluto is a true sign of Madonna's power. Her sheer force of being leads others to step out of the way. Lastly, Mercury conjunct Pluto speaks to Madonna's insightful and probing mind. Can this lady call the shots or what? And she's usually right, since she sees the big picture and can outsmart (or outshout?) the competition.

It's Venus in Leo which lets Madonna have so much fun in the game of love. Leo's presence here tells us this lady is highly attractive to the opposite sex and loves the romance dance. She won't hesitate to take risks with love, either. Since her Venus is square Neptune, the Planet of Illusion, however, Madonna is prone to viewing romance through rose-colored glasses. She's also fascinated with scandalous love affairs and will push the limits of her sexuality.

We can thank Mars in Taurus for the Material Girl's extra dose of stubbornness. With Taurus visiting the Planet of Passion, that nickname is no accident! Potent Mars also marks Madonna as self-assured where her values are concerned, even more so since the planet is in her Ninth House of Philosophy. The singer's exploration of Kabbalah enables her to get the answers she needs. Lastly, with Mars square Uranus, Madonna kicks things into overdrive. Umm, make that sex drive, since the Planet of Rebellion knows how to play.

Birth time source: Kepler

Other famous Leos:

Ben Affleck
Tori Amos
Gillian Anderson
Angela Bassett
Halle Berry
Bill Clinton
David Duchovny
Melanie Griffith
Woody Harrelson
Dustin Hoffman
Whitney Houston
Mick Jagger
Lisa Kudrow
Jennifer Lopez
Sean Penn
Robert Redford
Arnold Schwarzenegger
Christian Slater
Wesley Snipes
Billy Bob Thornton

VIRGO

Virgo: The Virgin

Any Virgos reading this are advised to lighten up. Don't get too picky or critical. Yes, we know you only want to make it better but — and therein lies the paradox of Virgo. While these folks may be known for their overweening fussiness, it's simply because they want to improve on everything that crosses their path. Virgo is known as the Sign of Service for a reason. Those born under this Sign are modest and efficient and simply can't help themselves when it comes to analyzing a situation and finding ways to make it better. Virgos have this technique down to a T.

Virgo rules the Sixth House, the House of Health. With all that fretting and correcting, Virgos are prime candidates for an ulcer or at least for a case of the nerves. However, the Virgin is also a serious student of health. Fastidious as they are, Virgos understand the benefits of hygiene, proper rest, and a good diet which may actually make them healthier than most. Understanding things and working from that point onward is the bedrock of the Virgo personality: these folks love to process. This is in keeping with the Mutable Quality which is assigned to this Sign. Virgos are practical, logical, and enjoy looking at a situation from every angle. They often do this quietly, though, since Virgos can be shy and reserved. But underneath, you can bet that it's processing central with all the circuits and wires going full-tilt. Zap. Pop. Bing! Yep, the Virgo's figured it out, yet again.

Virgos are great to have around because they're:
1. Neat
2. Organized
3. Particular

They're also a pain because they're:
1. Neat
2. Organized
3. Particular

Working with a Virgo nearby is always a good idea. You can consider them the Keeper of the List, since they'll always have at least one and likely several lists floating around. Lists of lists, cross-referenced as to priority and import. Virgos love organization and function best in a neat and clean environment. It's also a good bet that their head will be as organized as their surroundings. While they may use a Filofax to calendar appointments, most Virgos could just as easily carry this data around in their heads. And using their heads is a natural for these folks, since they are ruled by the Planet Mercury. As the Messenger God in ancient Roman mythology, Mercury probably didn't use a Filofax. He did, however, put his quick thinking and strong reasoning abilities to good use, much like Virgos do. Where information is concerned, Virgos feel best when they have a lot of it at hand, which is why they often probe a situation deeply. That way, they can feel comfortable that they're reaching the right conclusion. A bit compulsive? Well, Virgos would prefer to call it due diligence. Detailed. Precise.

Earthy Virgos are naturally associated with the Element of Earth. These folks have their feet firmly planted on the ground, the better to collect real data and analyze it — to death? Nah, Virgos don't generally go overboard, since they're basically practical creatures. Virgos are sensible folks who nonetheless know what they want, and this usually includes a few nice things. See, Virgos can be very discriminating and can spot Ming from Ping (vases, dahling) in an instant. And one Ming vase will do, since it's the quality that the Virgin's after, not gaudiness. Virgos carry this sensible slant into the business world as well, where they can spot a spotty deal a mile away. Those born under this Sign want to deal in sure things and real deals. Snake oil salesmen should take the first exit before reaching the Virgin, lest they be exposed for the frauds they are.

Not every Virgo wants a career as a Professional Organizer, though they could handle the job better than anyone. (Just look at a Virgo's closet, go ahead: all the shoes will be lined up and coordinated by color and season.) These folks realize they are neat, detailed, and discerning. They can take most any situation, break it into its component parts, and see where the real value is. What they want to do most of all, however, is to use these skills in the service of others. Virgos feel best when they are helping people and making a contribution to their world. The fact that they can fix things in the process is an added bonus.

With all this brain work going on, Virgos need to take time to recharge their batteries. These folks do enjoy sitting back and reading a book, but when it comes to physical exercise, they're much more interested in the benefits of a particular activity rather than the pleasure. How Virgo! Expect to find the Virgin on a treadmill or swimming laps as opposed to playing doubles tennis. When it comes to love, Virgos like to think first and smooch later, since the real attraction for them is between the ears.

The Virgo-born are particular, practical folks who love attention to detail and analyzing the specifics of a situation. They are also unassuming yet discriminating and enjoy being of service to others. What's sexy to a Virgo? Efficiency!

Sean Connery
BORN: AUGUST 25, 1930 6:05 PM EDINBURGH, SCOTLAND

It's no surprise that Virgo Sean Connery carries the weight of his years so well. The smooth Scottish actor was a bodybuilder as a young man — prep, he'd hoped, for a career as a professional soccer player. Sports were not to be his arena, though. Stumbling into acting in London between stints as a beefcake model, Connery played bit parts until he landed the role which would cement his career, that of suave agent 007 in the James Bond series. His first Bond flick was "Dr. No," followed by "Goldfinger," "You Only Live Twice," and "Diamonds are Forever," to name a few. Temporarily tiring of the Bond babefest, Connery switched to character roles in the 80s, playing a tough Irish cop in "The Untouchables" (an Oscar-winning role) and Indiana Jones's archaeologist pop in "Indiana Jones and the Last Crusade." Back for more action in "The Hunt for Red October" and "The Rock," Connery is proving well into his 60s that he's as dashing as ever!

Born with his Sun in Virgo, Connery is exacting and detail-oriented and won't shy away from a good day's work. On the job and off, the actor is likely to be a perfectionist, one who needs to get it right. Those ruled by Virgo tend to be picky and critical as well, although they'd tell you it was simply a matter of their discerning eye. Since Connery's Sun comes together with Neptune, the Planet of Make-Believe, he's a true chameleon, someone who could make you believe whatever he's willing to let you see. This placement is the sign of the actor, one who moves easily from one role to the next; it also suggests an individual who was not connected to a father figure.

With his Moon in Virgo as well, Connery's emotions take on a heavy Virgoan bent. Think practical, methodical, and efficient in the emotion department. Since the actor's Sun and Moon are both Earth Signs, expect him to be ultra-grounded and sure of his steps. No pie-in-the-sky or wishy-washy behavior here: the great Scot is all about order, efficiency, and a sensible nature. Call him smooth if you like, but he's certainly sure-footed! The Virgin is obviously in love with this man (can you blame her?) as Connery's Mercury, the Planet of Communication, is also in Virgo. This gives us a man who speaks well and has clear, logical thoughts. Connery is a director's dream, someone who will know his lines inside out and may even coach his colleagues on the set. With the considerable Virgo presence in his chart, it stands to reason that Connery is a perfectionist.

Saturn, the Planet of Hard Work and Discipline, is conjunct Connery's Rising Sign of Capricorn in the heavens. As the ruler of Capricorn, Saturn's placement here is the best of all possible worlds, since it adds extra emphasis to the qualities it projects. This Capricorn Ascendant allows Connery to present himself to the world as an ambitious and disciplined man and one who knows the value of hard work. Those graced by Capricorn in

Why is Sean Connery still sizzling well into his sixties?

Those graced by Capricorn on the Ascendant tend to get better the older they get — and it's Venus 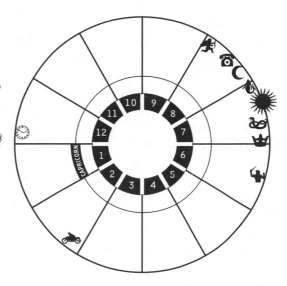 _in Libra which gives Connery his plentiful sex appeal._

their charts have a knack for getting better the older they get, and Connery's certainly done plenty of that! Suddenly, it's easy to see why Connery won his Oscar so late in the game, and why women will continue to swoon over this sexy man for years to come.

It's Venus in Libra which gives Connery that shiny patina. The Planet of Love and Beauty is merging with Libra, a Sign which lives for loveliness and a pleasant aesthetic. The actor will be charming and sociable as a result and a pleasure to look at. Since Venus is the ruler of Libra as well, the qualities of this Sign are emphasized, so Connery will work hard to maintain harmony and will always have the right thing to say. Yes, smooth indeed. Thanks to Mars in Gemini, however, Connery gets a bit of fire under his bum. His Planet of Passion pegs him as an intellectual, someone who enjoys a debate and will have a good grasp of the facts (all that Virgo helps). This quick thinker won't tolerate sloppiness and might choose a crossword puzzle or a game of Trivial Pursuit as a form of relaxation. Our man 007? Hey, how many babes can you chase?

A closer look at Connery's chart shows more planets in Earth Signs (Taurus, Virgo, Capricorn) than any other. Our man Bond is grounded, practical — and, oh yeah, materialistic. 007 wouldn't have it any other way!

Birth time source: Chryss Craswell, "BCAA"

Cameron Diaz

BORN: AUGUST 30, 1972 SAN DIEGO, CALIFORNIA USA

Sitting still was never in the picture for Virgo Cameron Diaz. The sun-kissed California girl saw modeling as the ticket to some big dreams, so she signed on with an agency at the age of sixteen. First stop? Japan. Diaz proceeded to travel to Europe, Australia, and other exciting locales over the next several years, ultimately deciding to go into acting when the mannequin's life got old. Scoring a role which many a more established actress craved as her first, Diaz shone opposite funnyman Jim Carrey in "The Mask." Choosing to go the indie route next, the blue-eyed blonde found herself at home (sort of) in "Feeling Minnesota" and played a schemer in "She's The One." Playing opposite Julia Roberts in the hit flick "My Best Friend's Wedding," Diaz showed she had spunk to spare and was destined for bigger films. Her hilarious schtick in the sleeper hit "There's Something About Mary" erased any doubts about Diaz being a big-time actress!

Born with her Sun in Virgo, Diaz is neat, precise, and a hard worker. Behind that pretty smile lies a discriminating woman who can veer toward perfectionism (and the pickiness that comes with it) quite easily. A good eye can turn into skepticism for Diaz, and she is prone to melancholy on her darker days. With her Sun conjunct (next to) Mars, our friend "Mary" is one hyper-focused individual. She'll arrive at the set on time and ready to go and expects the same from everyone else. Hey, this is part of this lady's finely-tuned career plan, one which could well take her to the top. On the flip side of things, Diaz's Sun is square Neptune, the Planet of Illusion. This alignment lends itself to dreaminess, unrealistic expectations, and even escapism. Although it's a good placement for an actor, too much time in this fantasy world will be counterproductive to Diaz's goals. Can you say conflicting celestial energies?

Thanks to her Mercury in Leo, the actress knows how to hold someone's attention. The Lion may be prone to exaggeration, but more often than not, Diaz will trade on her creative mental outlook and the ability to be dramatic with her ideas. Since Mercury is sextile Saturn in Gemini here, the Planet of Communication is making a favorable aspect to its own Sign (Gemini). As a result, Diaz will exhibit mental discipline, a structured thought process, and the follow-through that goes along with it, all supported by her Virgo Sun.

It's Venus in Cancer which marks our new Best Friend as the familial kind and someone who is very emotional in the name of love. Diaz believes in marriage and, thanks to the Crab, would love to have a home filled with kids. Further, Diaz is pegged as sensitive in love and craves security from her partner. With her Venus square Uranus in Libra (the Sign of Partnerships), however, the apple cart of love is tipping over, and not in Diaz's favor. Uranus's penchant for rebellion may lead the actress into a series of ill-fated relationships

What's behind Cameron Diaz's megawatt smile?

With both her Sun ☀ and Mars ♂ in Virgo, Diaz knows how to get things done. This discriminating lady wants perfection, too. Ordinary Joes need not apply! A Capricorn who's also intent on being the best might catch this lady's eagle eye.

and make it difficult for her to distinguish friendship from romantic love. In addition, since Venus rules Libra, it's squaring its own Sign here, a hard energy which will invariably lead to conflict where love is concerned.

Diaz's Mars in Virgo is further proof of this lady's efficiency. Order and details are of paramount importance to the actress, as is a system for getting things done. Will she disdain those who don't play her game? Count on it, since the Virgin is a Critical Miss. It's Jupiter in Sagittarius, though, which allows Diaz to paint with broader brushstrokes. The actress is a seeker of the truth thanks to this alignment and will see fit to take risks and learn life's lessons for this very reason. Luck is also in the mix here. With Jupiter making an out-of-sign square to Pluto (in Libra), money will come to Diaz, but only after hard work. Although she should do very well, she may never feel as if she has enough money or sufficient critical acclaim.

A final peek at Diaz's chart shows Saturn in Gemini. This placement can curb the expression of ideas, although in Diaz's case, it's somewhat lightened up by Saturn's sextile to Mercury in Leo. With Saturn also trine Uranus, Diaz is new and fresh, granting her the ability to take what's old and traditional and give it a Gen X spin.

Birth time source: not available. As a result, references to the Rising Sign, Moon, and Houses may be omitted from this profile.

Gloria Estefan
BORN: SEPTEMBER 1, 1957 HAVANA, CUBA

The Latin pop scene found its Queen in Virgo Gloria Estefan, although the singer's humble beginnings belie her current state of grace. Born in Havana, Cuba, Estefan's parents fled the Castro regime and resettled in Miami in 1959 with little Gloria in tow. Painfully shy, the psych major decided to join a local band nonetheless as a way to indulge her love of music. Fronted by her future husband, Emilio Estefan, the Miami Sound Machine garnered rave reviews for its infectious Latin beat. The band's first English-language effort, 1985's "Primitive Love," rose to the top of the pop charts on the strength of the hit single "Conga." Deciding to pin its fortunes on their lead singer, the Sound Machine dropped its name and played backup to Estefan. The singer's first "solo" effort, "Cuts Both Ways," established her as a star in her own right. Although she suffered a serious back injury in a bus accident in 1990, the resilient Estefan bounced back within a year and continues to tour (and record) in both English and her native Spanish.

Born with her Sun in Virgo, Estefan is industrious, methodical, and dedicated. The singer will put in the extra effort required to get things just right and expects those around her to do the same. Those born under this Sign are discriminating and prefer to live within high standards. On the flip side of things, Virgos can be picky and critical to an excessive degree. That said, Estefan is modest about her successes and sees her work as truly important. With her Sun conjunct Mars, boldness and assertion will be part of Gloria's plan. This songstress's power reaches to the heroic thanks to a double dose of physical strength (that miraculous recovery after the bus accident is a perfect example). Estefan is blessed with initiative, will not hesitate to take action, and gets the job done. Estefan's Sun is also square Saturn, the Planet of Discipline. Somber Saturn tends to restrict the warmth of the Sun, rendering Estefan somewhat cold and reserved and making it harder for her to reach out to others. This aspect further speaks to a serious work ethic. Lastly, with the Sun conjunct Pluto, the Planet of Raw Power, opposing energies are at play. Pluto's power is met by the Sun's spunk and the result is a standoff. Estefan will either be very good or very bad, but there's no doubting that she will be very powerful.

With her Moon in Sagittarius, the lyrical Latina is both fluid and adaptable, although others might consider her a bit far out. The Archer in the sphere of emotions is a never-ending adventure, which is just how these people like it. Estefan will enjoy her freedom and considers the truth to be of paramount importance. She will also make friends easily and prefers to feel (and deal with) life through her experiences.

It's Mercury in Virgo as well which pegs the singer as precise and logical in her communications. Practical ideas will appeal to this woman and she'll revel in all sorts of fancy

Why does Gloria Estefan adhere to such high standards?

With her Sun ☀ in Virgo (as are Mercury and Mars), it's nothing but the best for golden Glo. The hardworking singer is both perceptive and discriminating and feels best when things pass her stringent litmus test. Scorpions know how to get to the finish line, which is why Estefan would be smitten with them.

facts and trivial details. The singer also picks things up quickly, so expect rehearsals to be a study in efficiency. With her Venus in pretty Libra, golden Glo wants love to be a beautiful affair. The singer will work toward congenial relations and will do everything in her power to create a happy marriage. Expect Estefan's tastes to be rather refined and for her to indulge her love of luxury. With her Venus unaspected in the heavens (making no aspect to any other planet), Estefan is likely to make her own rules in the game of love.

Passionate Mars is visiting perfunctory Virgo in Estefan's chart, a surefire sign of orderly behavior. The singer will work best within a system, and she's probably happy to let manager/husband Emilio design it so that she can execute it. Virgo's kinship with Mars here also signals middling sexual energy — look for the singer's marriage to be more about projects than passion.

A closer look at Estefan's chart shows Jupiter, the Planet of Luck, in Libra, the mark of just and principled behavior. The singer will also be lucky in both her personal and business relationships. Lastly, with Saturn in Sagittarius, Miami's sound machine is pegged as a seeker of the truth. The fact that this planet is trine Uranus further tells us that Estefan is a humanitarian who is ahead of her time.

Birth time source: not available. As a result, references to the Rising Sign, Moon, and Houses may be omitted from this profile.

Richard Gere

BORN: AUGUST 31, 1949 PHILADELPHIA, PENNSYLVANIA USA

He may look awfully good in that designer suit, but Virgo Richard Gere wasn't always so slick. Raised in rural New York, Gere gravitated toward the stage early on and toured in small productions before heading to New York City. After a stint on Broadway, the actor turned his attention to the big screen. Working with highly-regarded director Terrence Malick on "Days of Heaven," Gere showed the world he could act. Playing with the ladies in "American Gigolo," the actor proved he had mass appeal. With the success of "An Officer and a Gentleman," Gere chose to leverage his newfound fame on behalf of the Dalai Lama and the disenfranchised of Tibet. This devout Buddhist founded the Tibet House in New York and uses every opportunity to present his case. Enjoying a surge in popularity after the release of "Pretty Woman" in 1990, Gere proceeded to marry a pretty woman of his own, supermodel Cindy Crawford. While the marriage wasn't nearly as successful as the movie (the couple divorced after four years), Gere's on- and off-screen passions are still in full swing.

Born with his Sun in Virgo, Gere is a man who forever wants to get things right. As befits the Sign of Service, the actor prefers to take on projects which prove useful (his efforts for Tibet fill the bill) and is dutiful in that which he undertakes. Known for their exacting behavior, Virgos can be picky and critical, though one can choose to see this as discriminating and analytical. That's certainly how Virgos see it! Since his Sun is conjunct Saturn, the Planet of Discipline, Gere's sense of duty and penchant for hard work is redoubled. While the actor may be tough on others, he's toughest on himself. With both his Sun and Saturn sextile Uranus, the Planet of Rebellion, expect Gere to take things which are outside the mainstream and make them current (can you say Buddhism?). The Sun's sextile to Uranus speaks to personal charisma and a search for answers while Saturn's sextile to Uranus addresses the push/pull between freedom and discipline. The sum total here is that while Gere will not be bound by conventions, he's pragmatic enough to get the job done.

With his Moon in Sagittarius, the philosopher in Gere comes to the fore. The actor's *raison d'être* is the search for meaning. Restless by nature, Gere craves freedom, and this quest for space lends itself to travel. Along with physical independence, the actor requires emotional independence and can't stand anyone dictating to him. High ideals are also part of the actor's makeup, as is a blunt and straightforward approach.

It's Mercury in Libra which gives Gere that smooth-talking sensibility. The Scales love being fair and just, a quality which might lead to indecision. To his credit, though, Gere can ebb and flow with inimitable grace and can be persuasive when need be. Since his Mercury is square Uranus, however, Gere won't always say what others want to hear. What's more, he won't even care! Uranus speaks to radical ideas and unconventional thought, and although Libra endeavors to put a sweet spin on things, Gere's manner will often be difficult.

Why is Richard Gere forever searching for meaning?

Thanks to his Sagittarius Moon **☾**, the one-time American Gigolo is truly Zen. Restless by nature, Gere may well travel the world looking for answers to everything. In the love department, a Taurean will be the answer to this man's prayers.

Thanks to Venus in Libra as well, the American Gigolo likes a pleasing aesthetic in the name of love. Harmony in relationships (marriage included) is what the actor seeks, and he'll go about this in a refined and extravagant way. With Venus conjunct Neptune, the Planet of Illusion, Gere is almost spiritual about love and is prone to idealizing his relationship and his lover. Ever the romantic, the actor may not be very practical when in love and can easily set himself up for disappointment. Since Venus is sextiling Pluto, though, Gere is charismatic with the ladies and will attract them with ease.

Gere's Mars in Cancer marks this gentleman as moody and emotional — about anything and everything. The Planet of Passion unleashes powerful tears from Gere, and he won't even mind. Mars is struggling here, too, since this planet doesn't cozy up to the crabby Crab. While Mars is about action, the Crab would rather hide in its shell. The upshot is halting action at best; expect Gere to chafe under criticism and to seek solace among family and friends. With Mars opposite Jupiter, however, Gere gets a much-needed jolt. His physicality is reinforced, and the actor will find the strength to take risks.

A last look at Gere's chart shows Jupiter, the Planet of Good Fortune, in hardworking Capricorn. Bottom line: the actor is practical in business matters and good with money. Luck at the "office" should be his!

Birth time source: not available. As a result, references to the Rising Sign, Moon, and Houses may be omitted from this profile.

Other famous Virgos:

Lauren Bacall
Harry Connick, Jr.
David Copperfield
Hugh Grant
Salma Hayek
Michael Jackson
Tommy Lee Jones
Michael Keaton
Stephen King
Ricki Lake
Sophia Loren
Bill Murray
Jason Priestley
Keanu Reeves
LeAnn Rimes
Adam Sandler
Claudia Schiffer
Jada Pinkett Smith
Jonathan Taylor Thomas
Raquel Welch

LIBRA

Libra: The Scales

Okay, you're having a Libra over for cocktails: break out the crystal. And it had better be Baccarat. Those Librans — they do have an eye for what's nice. Librans want to live in a beautiful world, a place where peace and harmony prevail. Hey, their symbol is the Scales, remember? It's all about balance with Librans. No shrill friends, no messy spouses, no whiny kids. Everyone should be happy, pleasant, and balanced. That way Libra will be happy, too. The Libran's happy land, however, isn't complete without someone to share it with, which is why these folks are usually in the company of others. Why do you think Librans are regulars at cocktail parties? They work at perfecting their charming and sociable natures so that there will always be someone around, preferably a mate.

Libra rules the Seventh House, the House of Partnership. Librans are interested in creating a beautiful world not for the sake of finery, but so that everyone in it will feel good. That done, they will have earned the affection of others. And Librans do want to be loved, especially by that special someone. Marriage is a natural state for these folks, and it is likely to be a harmonious union since Librans will work hard to keep the peace. Much like the Scales of Justice they represent, Librans will bend over backwards to be fair, although at times they'll do so simply to avoid conflict. This can lead to accusations of being non-confrontational and indecisive, which will be true. That said, the Libran's primary goal will be to see all sides of a situation in order to arrive at a fair compromise. In business, Librans enjoy working with a group and can easily spearhead a project. This is in keeping with the Cardinal Quality assigned to this Sign. A Libran at work can be a pretty determined individual, eager to get ahead and to succeed. Charming as they are, if they can't dazzle 'em with brilliance, they'll baffle 'em with...

Librans usually shop at:
1. Saks
2. Tiffanys
3. Cartier

Librans are ruled by the Planet Venus, the Goddess of Love, Beauty, and Pleasure. This helps to explain that love of luxury and sheer, unadulterated pleasure in blessed excess. For this reason, Librans are wise to marry up. Unless they're rich already. The Libran home is likely to be filled with lovely things. Even moderately-heeled Librans will have a few choice possessions which are heavenly. The Scales generally know when enough is enough, but they will, on occasion, get carried away. How many diamond rings does a Libran need, anyway? Don't ask. The Libran's appreciation of beauty also translates to the arts, so expect to find these folks at museums, the opera, or the symphony. They also enjoy hosting small dinner parties where their gift for conversation will mesmerize their guests. The food will taste (and look) good, too. It's worth noting that Librans are also good listeners, since they are truly interested in others. Plus, they're flirts! Librans who don't bat their eyelashes can be counted on one hand.

The Element associated with Libra is Air, which means that these folks are intellectually-inclined. Their skill at wordplay is unsurpassed, except by the occasional smooth talker. While others will talk for the sake of talking, Librans, however, are more interested in saying the right thing. Enter the diplomat of the Zodiac — someone who knows how to make everyone feel good. (Remember those cocktail parties?) Librans are also keenly interested in learning about other people, places, and things. And when it comes to their intended, they'd much rather talk for hours on end before proceeding to the boudoir. Ah yes, words as foreplay are what the Libra craves.

While Librans love to talk, they hate to argue, so much so, that they might cave in to a ridiculous position simply to keep the peace. They can also doubt themselves from time to time. Fortunately, Librans can usually rally with a persuasive statement which is delivered so winningly that critics will choose to step aside. Librans rarely get angry, far preferring a kinder, gentler approach to life. They are also loyal and fair and believe that most situations can be handled in a spirit of truth, justice, and cooperation.

Librans see sports and recreation as yet another opportunity to socialize. "Let's go to the Club," they'll proclaim as they pack their tennis bag for yet another set of doubles. Libran golfers may be fondest of the 19th Hole, comparing scores and their vacation homes on the shore. The Scales, however, can be lazy, so they may need their mate to get them up and out of the house. In the game of love, Librans are romantic and playful and respond (not-so-surprisingly) well to gifts.

The Libra-born are lovers of beauty who prefer to channel their charm and energy toward their relationships with others. They are sociable and diplomatic and live for a world filled with peace and harmony. So what if their approach includes a wink and a smile? It works!

Matt Damon

BORN: OCTOBER 8, 1970 3:22 PM BOSTON, MASSACHUSETTS USA

Keeping your eye on the prize is one way to get what you want. Libra Matt Damon wanted to act from an early age, so he did just that. He had a partner in crime, too: neighborhood pal Ben Affleck. The young men scored bit parts in and around their Boston environs and even trekked to the Big Apple. Taking on minor roles while studying at Harvard (and majoring in English), Damon decided to make for L.A. before the diploma came in. The likable actor's big break came in "Courage Under Fire," a 1996 Army flick which cast him opposite Meg Ryan and Denzel Washington. His performance helped Damon land the lead in a John Grisham pic, "The Rainmaker." The Grisham glow propelled this young actor into Hollywood's back rooms where his (and Affleck's) script about a brilliant but tormented wannabe MIT man became "Good Will Hunting." The small film earned big box office thanks to its winning leading man, excellent casting (Robin Williams in an Oscar-winning role), and tight script. The latter earned an Academy Award for Damon and partner-in-crime Affleck. Having a winning way with the ladies as well (Claire Danes, Minnie Driver, and Winona Ryder are all in his little black book), Damon is cruising!

Born with his Sun in Libra, Damon is harmonious, peace-loving, and revels in the comforts of a relationship. He has a keen sense of the aesthetic (yes, those perfect teeth!), a refined bearing, and is most companionable. Matt at a cocktail party? You bet. Ever diplomatic, his penchant for good will, however, can lead to indecision, the hallmark of those to-and-fro Scales. A wrinkle in Damon's celestial plan is the fact that his Sun is conjunct Uranus, the Planet of Rebellion. Suddenly, Damon isn't a typical Libran. Uranus, as the ruler of the actor's Sun, is a powerful force. Don't be fooled by all the Libran prettiness — there's a lot going on underneath! Since Damon's Sun, Uranus, and Mercury are all intercepted in the Eighth House (of Sex, no less), the stud's intense energy is kept well hidden.

With his Moon in Capricorn, the rainmaker is just that: a hardworking man who is ambitious, determined, and driven to succeed. That his feelings can appear a bit cold at times is part of the plan. The Moon, which naturally rules Cancer, finds itself visiting its opposite Sign, Capricorn, here. In a word (or two): difficult combo. The harsh energy being sent forth speaks to one who is aloof, controlled, and exceedingly cautious. Further, expect Damon to tie his emotional security to his material wealth. With his Moon in the Twelfth House, the House of the Surreal, our trusty scribe is further stifled where his emotions are concerned. Although intuitive, Damon will have a hard time reaching out to others. Part of this difficulty may be rooted in his Moon's square to the Sun. This alignment indicates conflicts at home which have shut Damon off from others emotionally. In essence, the actor may not be dealing with childhood issues which still haunt him. "Good Will Hunting" may be truer than we know.

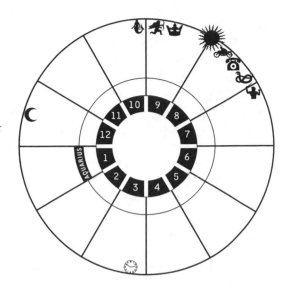

Why does Matt Damon look at love through rose-colored glasses?
With comely Venus ♐ sitting next to Neptune ♆ in the heavens, romance is illusory for the handsome actor.

It's a Rising Sign of Aquarius which gives Damon his mischievous spin. The actor certainly appears to be his own man, an individual who could border between genius and insanity (as ruler Uranus would have it). Once again, "Good Will" and his brilliant mind could easily be this man's alter ego. Damon may be seen as unpredictable but is quickly redeemed by his altruistic demeanor. Thanks to Mercury in Libra (and next to powerful Pluto), Damon will get his message across beautifully, and forcefully at that. Consequently, that screenwriting Oscar is no surprise.

Damon's Venus, the Planet of Love, is keeping company with Scorpio here, making for one hot tamale in the love department. With his Venus conjunct Neptune, however, Damon may have a knack for seeing all that sass in the sack through rose-colored glasses. Having his Venus opposite Saturn in Taurus makes things even harsher. Venus's sociability finds itself at odds with Saturn's aloofness, making it difficult for Damon to reach out to his lover. His relationships may well suffer, and marriage certainly appears to be a dicey proposition.

Marvelous Matt finds his Mars, the Planet of Passion, in Virgo and conjunct Pluto, the proponent of sheer force. Virgo's critical bent kicks into overtime here, rendering Damon a nitpicker of the first order. All work and no play may be Matt's mantra, but this Libran should leave time for some fun in between.

Birth time source: Aspects Magazine, Summer '98, "BC AA"

Susan Sarandon

BORN: OCTOBER 4, 1946 2:25 PM NEW YORK, NEW YORK USA

Are Catholic school girls the fairest of them all? Perhaps, especially if you consider that Libran Susan Sarandon was so schooled, although that rigid tutelage did nothing to sub-due the actress's sexy mood. Sarandon was also an activist early on and harbored a desire to be on stage. Kicking around between Broadway, movies, and TV, the actress compiled a creditable resume, although she didn't capture much attention until her quirky turn as Janet in the cult flick "The Rocky Horror Picture Show." Appearing in "Pretty Baby" and "Atlantic City" soon afterward, Sarandon proved that she could headline more mainstream films. By the time she appeared as Annie Savoy, the saucy baseball groupie in "Bull Durham," Sarandon's star was firmly in place. This film also served to introduce Sarandon to her longtime companion, actor/director Tim Robbins. Her subsequent per-formances in "Thelma and Louise" and "The Client" were mere prelude to Sarandon's career role as Sister Helen Prejean in "Dead Man Walking," the role which finally won the actress an Oscar under the direction of Robbins.

Born with her Sun in Libra, Sarandon is charming, diplomatic, and a lover of beauty. Graced by the Scales, the actress wants harmony in her life and knows that cooperation and teamwork will help her get it. Socially-inclined and refined Librans also crave com-panionship and feel best when in a relationship. With her Sun conjunct Neptune in the Eighth House of Sex, Sarandon is a master at changing roles. Since Scorpio rules the Eighth House, the accent is on sexy role play, so it's easy for Sarandon to pull from with-in to create these personae. The Eighth House influencing her Libra Sun also signals financial benefits through partnership for the actress.

Thanks to her Moon in Capricorn (and sitting on her Ascendant), the actress's emotions may appear stern and almost business-like. This is a challenging placement in Sarandon's chart: the Moon, being female energy, doesn't take kindly to Capricorn's macho-CEO mentality. The result is subdued emotions and a cautious, even serious outlook on things. Expect Sarandon to need money to feel good and to have a somewhat materialistic bent. Since her Rising Sign is also in Capricorn, our friend "Louise" will appear exactly how she feels: detached, organized, and materialistic. One will always see the ambition which burns within this lady; Sarandon will also appear self-possessed and in control.

It's her Mercury, the Planet of Communication, in Libra which marks the actress as an intellectual who is a good talker and knows how (and when) to say the right thing. Tact and a clever sense will also come easily to Sarandon thanks to Libra's glow. Since Mercury is making an out-of-sign conjunction to Jupiter in Scorpio here (in the Ninth House of Philosophy), look for Sarandon to be a clear thinker who embraces both tangible and

What's the key to Susan Sarandon's long-lived career?

The sultry actress has passionate Mars ♏ in Scorpio, a surefire sign of willpower and determination. Sex, money, fame — it's hers if she wants it, and her lust for life tells us she does!

abstract concepts. Since this conjunction is afflicted, however, she could become enamored of her own words, especially in the areas of religion and spirituality. Convinced that she's right, the actress might even be inclined to be dogmatic. It should also be noted that with Mars nearby, Sarandon won't hesitate to put her thoughts, and words, into action.

With her Venus in Scorpio at the top of her chart (conjunct the M.C.), Sarandon is quick to put her plentiful sexuality front and center. No shy Di here! This is a woman who is passionate in love, shrewd with money (and she also seems to attract riches), and vengeful if betrayed. Further, Sarandon is attractive to both men and women, and once she sets her mind to something (someone?), that's it. Since her Venus is on the M.C., Sarandon's public image and reputation are stellar, and success should surely be hers.

Sarandon's Mars, the Planet of Passion, is also visited by the Scorpion. A word of warning: mess with this woman at your own risk! The actress has the drive and sheer will to get what she wants, and if it's money, no problem, since Scorpio is the Sign of Finance. If Sarandon turns her sights on sex, no problem there, either, since the Scorpion in the Planets of Love and Passion speaks to sexual abandon. With her Mars conjunct Jupiter, the Planet of Luck, look for Sarandon to be doubly blessed where money, and sex, are concerned. Since Mars is also square Saturn and Pluto here, Sarandon could make short work of the competition but will still come out smiling.

Birth time source: Lois Rodden

Will Smith

BORN: SEPTEMBER 25, 1968 PHILADELPHIA, PENNSYLVANIA USA

Can rap be anything but gangsta-speak? Take a listen to Libran Will Smith, a homeboy (though he grew up middle-class) who sounds anything but mean. This Philly kid was a music hound from early on and started making rap music in his teens. Success was assured once Smith teamed up with boyhood pal Jeff "DJ Jazzy Jeff" Townes, since these tunesters knew how to groove a mood. The Grammys and other awards which followed only served to whet Smith's appetite for bigger things. Moving on to TV, the show "Fresh Prince of Bel Air" was tailor-made for the rapper, as it depicted a Philly kid (sound familiar?) who found himself in the Hollywood Hills. The Quincy Jones-produced show ran for six years, after which Smith hit the big screen. "Six Degrees of Separation," a dark 1993 film, cast Smith as the gay, wannabe son of Sidney Poitier. The film led to Smith's breakout role as a funny yet bold fighter pilot who saves the world in the blockbuster "Independence Day." With the "Men in Black" movie and soundtrack equally big successes and his solo effort, "Big Willie Style" yet another hit, Smith and his wife, actress Jada Pinkett, are one of Tinseltown's hottest couples.

Born with his Sun in Libra, Smith is personable, cooperative, and just, which sounds about right for the even-handed Scales. The Fresh Prince, as befits his regal nom de tune, is refined and gracious. Hmmm, make that suave in the sweetest of ways — no slick Willie here! Although the rapper is forever the diplomat, he can be fickle and indecisive at times. In keeping with Libra's penchant for partnerships, Smith will feel best when in a relationship, which may explain his two marriages by the age of thirty. Since his Sun is conjunct Uranus and Pluto, the rapper marches to his own drummer. This conjunction also pegs Smith as a powerful individual, someone who can leverage his unique appeal to maximum advantage.

With his Moon in Scorpio, Smith's force field is strengthened. And you thought the "Men in Black" were tough? Think again, since this MIB is a cyclone in the emotional realm. Smith's intense energies mark him as someone to be reckoned with, a man who gets down to business and abhors the superficial. The actor would also love it if his mate shared this trait.

It's Mercury, the Planet of Communication, in Libra which ensures that Smith will say the right thing. This smooth talker is also smart about what he says and can be subtly persuasive, making those CD sales no fluke. With his Mercury conjunct Venus, the Planet of Love (in Libra as well), the actor's gift of glib translates to the ladies, too. Expect Smith to be the consummate conversationalist, someone who is good-natured, friendly, and popular to boot. As for pillow talk, it's a sho' thang!

Why is Will Smith so suave?

With his Sun ☀, Mercury ☎, and Venus ♐ all in diplomatic Libra, the Fresh Prince is smooth as silk, and he always plays fair. Princely, indeed! The thinking person's rapper, Smith feeds off of Gemini's mercurial mental energy when putting together a new groove.

Smith's Venus in Libra marks him as truly dignified, a quality reinforced by his Libran Sun. This man wants congenial relations, period, so a happy marriage would suit him to a "T." Libra's energy further ensures that Smith will be easy on the eyes, and a pleasing aesthetic is sure to keep him in the pink (a beautiful home is a foregone conclusion). With both his Mercury and Venus opposite Saturn in Aries, we see the actor has worked hard at being a class act. While Mercury's opposition to Saturn tells us Smith may feel self-conscious in conversation and disdains social chitchat, Venus's opposition to the Planet of Discipline speaks to Smith's difficulty in reaching out in love. Smith's best moments are when he's hard at work and looking good — that's Big Willie Style!

Thanks to his Mars in Virgo, the rapper's Passion Planet commands him to nitpick. The efficiency and orderliness of the Virgin is emphasized, and the result is one who approaches things in a meticulous and systematic way. With Mars and Venus making an out-of-sign sextile (60-degree angle) here, the actor tends to be warm and affectionate with others, especially those he loves. He relates easily to the opposite sex and works well in partnership (a quality supported by Smith's Libra Sun).

A final look at Smith's chart shows a preponderance of Earth planets, marking Big Willie as a man with a plan. He'll stick with it too, so there's much more in store from this Philly kid!

Birth time source: not available. As a result, references to the Rising Sign, Moon, and Houses may be omitted from this profile.

Sigourney Weaver
BORN: OCTOBER 8, 1949 6:15 PM NEW YORK, NEW YORK USA

The former Susan Weaver probably never imagined herself an alien growing up. Libran Sigourney Weaver (how's that for jazzing up your name?) was a child of privilege on the East Coast, thanks to her Dad's cushy job as President of NBC. Even so, Weaver grew up the rebel, having a taste of the hippie movement while she padded between Stanford and Yale. The acting bug finally bit, and this actress proceeded to show the world how seamlessly she could flit between action, comedy, and drama. As uberwoman Ripley in "Alien," Weaver proved the point that outer space wasn't just for the boys. Switching to comedy for a while, this leading lady showed her sass in "Ghostbusters" and "Working Girl." One of Weaver's finest dramatic turns was in the role of anthropologist Dian Fossey in "Gorillas in the Mist;" her performance as the icy Mom in Ang Lee's "The Ice Storm" was also critically acclaimed. Weaver's best cinematic trick, however, may have been in the fourth installment of the "Alien" series, "Alien Resurrection," in which she managed to bring back Ripley from her death in "Alien 3."

Born with her Sun in Libra, Weaver is keen on living in a harmonious world. To that end, she is cooperative, persuasive, and peace-loving. Those graced by Libra tend to be refined and artistic and are always the most charming and sociable folks in a room. Any East Coast soirees in her early days were tailor-made for this lady! While diplomatic in nature, Librans can also be fickle and indecisive. They do always manage, however, to consider the feelings of others.

With both her Moon and Rising Sign in Taurus, the actress has a Bullish bent which makes her both plodding and stubborn. Where her Moon is concerned, the Taurean marker signals a touchy-feely woman whose emotions are nonetheless steady. Weaver's emotional makeup is affectionate and loyal, especially since she places great value on her parents, home, and family. The Taurean-aligned also value financial security and enjoy material comforts. It's interesting to note that Weaver's Moon sits right on top of her Ascendant. We can glean that Weaver will wear her heart on her sleeve and will be focused on how others see her. What you see is what you get with this woman!

It's Mercury in Libra which once again puts a sleek slant on things. Weaver's Planet of Communication is visiting the Scales, who love to talk. In keeping with that all-important balancing act, Weaver will also be a good mediator and ever-focused on keeping the peace. She also has a knack for saying the right thing. Since Libra is ruled by Venus, expect Weaver to look good, stand tall (no problem there), and make nice. Venus herself happens to be visiting Scorpio in Weaver's chart, a placement which gives the actress her sizzle and spark. The Planet of Love is getting Scorpionic energy here, so look for an

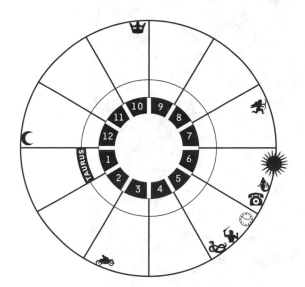

What gives Sigourney Weaver an almost superhuman strength?
With Weaver's Mars 🦁 *sitting next to Pluto* ♇*, the Planet of Raw Power, the actress is fearless, bold, and powerful, much like her alter ego Ripley in the "Alien" series.*

intense, passionate woman in the love department who won't be afraid of being sexy! Scorpio's force field may make for some stormy relationships (that "ice storm" may not have been totally out of character), so it would be unwise to betray this lady.

Thanks to Mars in Leo, Weaver knows how to get things done. Now we see how Ripley came back from the dead! Weaver has the will to overcome long odds and the confidence to succeed in any arena. She's also ambitious and a born leader (our favorite alien is clearly cast to type). An extra dose of energy comes as a result of Weaver's Mars in Leo being conjunct, or next to, Pluto, the Planet of Raw Power. When these two come together, look out. Think driving ambition and an almost superhuman strength. Weaver is fearless, bold, and powerful, much like her alter ego in the "Alien" series. Her magnetic personality will attract others, whom she may choose to rule with an iron fist. Whew!

Looking at Weaver's chart a bit further, one sees her Sun conjunct Neptune, the Planet of Make-Believe. This association is the mark of an actor. Lastly, Weaver's Jupiter is in Capricorn at the top of her chart (also known as the M.C.). This placement speaks to luck and good fortune in her career as a result of her hard work. Jupiter's fortuitous energy will likely lead to accolades for the actress and the respect of her peers.

Birth time source: Pathfinder: John Woodsmall

Other famous Librans:

Brigitte Bardot
Toni Braxton
Neve Campbell
Michael Douglas
Sarah Ferguson
Carrie Fisher
Heather Locklear
Gwyneth Paltrow
Luciano Pavarotti
Luke Perry
Christopher Reeve
Anne Rice
Tim Robbins
Alicia Silverstone
Mira Sorvino
Bruce Springsteen
Sting
Jean-Claude Van Damme
Barbara Walters
Kate Winslet

SCORPIO

Scorpio: The Scorpion

Scorpio is the Sign of Sex and Death. Oooh, and just when that was starting to sound so promising! Those born under this Sign would probably prefer to concentrate on the former (and they do), but they can't seem to get away from the latter. Hey, none of us can in the end; it's just that Scorpios seem to wallow in death a bit more than most. It all starts with that pesky little Scorpion, a critter that would rather kill itself than be killed. Great. On top of that, the Scorpion can lose its tail and grow a new one. Okay, death, regeneration, rebirth. Scorpios are pretty comfortable with endings and new beginnings. These fearless folks are the probers of the Zodiac, eager to discover the motivations of others and what makes them tick. They're investigative and penetrative, and they're none too subtle about it. The Scorpion's new friends are going to have to pass their litmus test, and they'd better get an "A".

Scorpio rules the Eighth House which is (what else?) the House of Sex. As the most sexual of the twelve Signs, these folks can do the tango fandango with the best of 'em, but it all starts long before that. Ever had a Scorpion look you in the eye? Those eyes are like laser beams looking right through you. Zap. You are toast, bubba. The Scorpion owns you. Those born under this Sign are strong-willed and determined and love to win, both in the bedroom and the boardroom. And you'll never find them in the bored-room, since these folks will take on a project and won't let go until victory is theirs. This is also in keeping with the Fixed Quality associated with this Sign. Scorpions like doing things their way, making "my way or the highway" their mantra in life. This isn't necessarily a bad thing, however, since Scorpios are quick to consider the interests of the community or a particular group. When entrusted with the assets of others, they will usually do a top notch job, thanks in no small part to their killer instinct. Yes, death plays into it once again.

Role models for Scorpions include:
1. Rambo
2. 007
3. Roseanne

The Scorpion is ruled by two planets, Mars and Pluto. Mars is the Planet of War and Pluto is the Planet of the Underworld. If you aren't scared yet, you should be. Scorpions tend to adopt a take-no-prisoners attitude to life, doing what needs to be done to accomplish their goals. These folks also make for excellent tacticians and are possessed of an iron will which comes in handy in the field of battle. Hmm, make that life. The Scorpion's maneuvers can be unsettling to some, since these folks won't hesitate to be mysterious, secretive, or blunt if it will help them achieve their objectives. A Scorpion tip their hand?

Forget it. These folks are poker players *par excellence,* and if you never really know what the Scorpion is up to, that's exactly how they want it. In all fairness to Scorpios, though, they can be pretty deep behind all that bluster. They want to know what motivates others, and they are highly intuitive in this regard. It's just that with Scorpions, nothing is half way. They won't engage you in small talk — they'll question and probe until they know more about you than you do.

The Element associated with Scorpions is Water, marking them as an emotional Sign. Huh? Okay, consider them repressed emotions where Scorpios are concerned since much of what goes on with these folks is behind the scenes. Scorpions can be perceptive to the point of arrogance, knowing they've got your number and taking their time while they decide what to do with that information. Best to keep these folks on your good side just in case. That said, Scorpions are loyal to those who have proven their worth and their honor. They don't suffer fools gladly, but then who should?

The myth of the Phoenix who rises from the ashes is a good parallel for the Scorpion. After all, both creatures are practiced in the art of regeneration. Scorpios are good at reinventing themselves, taking ordinary circumstances and questing for the extraordinary. They love a challenge, a quality which translates to the physical as well. These folks won't play a game for the heck of it: they are in it to win. See to it that the Scorpion is always on your team. Where love is concerned, Scorpions can be caring and devoted, and their magnetism will prove hard to resist, regardless of the circumstances. Since Scorpio rules the reproductive organs, expect these folks to spend a lot of time thinking about sex, too. A Scorpion on a hot date is likely to be dressed in red and black, colors as intense and lusty as they are.

The Scorpio-born are passionate and determined and have what it takes to be a winner. They are strong-willed, sometimes unconventional, and always intense. Since they tend to see things as black or white, play it safe and have them on your side!

Leonardo DiCaprio

BORN: NOVEMBER 11, 1974 2:47 AM LOS ANGELES, CALIFORNIA USA

Is he a titanic actor or merely a pretty face? Scorpio Leonardo DiCaprio might answer yes to the former, while his legion of (mostly female) fans would surely affirm both. Despite his monumental press for the film "Titanic" and the undying love of many a lass, the actor has earned his cinematic stripes. Taking roles early on with the support of his parents, DiCaprio's first taste of success came on the TV sitcom "Growing Pains." He parlayed this recognition into movie roles, catching the eye of many in "This Boy's Life" opposite Robert De Niro. Playing Johnny Depp's sweet and simple brother in "What's Eating Gilbert Grape?" DiCaprio was able to establish that he could do much more than simply look good; he followed this up with a wrenching performance in "The Basketball Diaries." These triumphs, however, paled in comparison to his turn as king of the world in James Cameron's megahit "Titanic." Though he wasn't favored with an Academy Award nomination for his performance in that film (and skipped the Awards altogether), DiCaprio has a lot of acting left in him

Born with his Sun in Scorpio, DiCaprio is, above all, intense. Despite his tender age, he has the ability to pull from within when creating a role. He is also probing and mysterious and demonstrates unswerving courage. Much of his sex appeal can be attributed to his Scorpionic Sun, a surefire sign of sexual energy. Those born under this Sign are also fearless and plow into anything that will promote their agenda. Leo may look as sweet as pie, but it would be a big mistake to cross this fellow.

Thanks to his Moon in Libra, DiCaprio's persona is softened up. Libra's aversion to disharmony and discord serves the actor well, and he will want to make peace if at all possible. He will also exhibit the social graces necessary to achieve that end. With his Moon conjunct, or next to, Pluto, the Power Planet, DiCaprio's emotions are a force field of activity. The actor will sense weakness in others and use this to his advantage. This penchant for control is also present in his relationships with women. A pricklier aspect in DiCaprio's chart is the fact that this conjunction is afflicted by Saturn, the Planet of Hard Work and Responsibility. This hard aspect results in a very strong energy; DiCaprio expects nothing but the best from those around him and gives zero ground on anything. Since it's the Moon we're talking about here, DiCaprio is likely to practice his prickliness on women.

With his Rising Sign also in Libra, titanic "Jack" comes across as sociable, charming, and a lover of the aesthetic. His paintings of "Rose" in that waterlogged film weren't much of a stretch! With Pluto bearing down on his Ascendant, however, the pretty picture won't last for long. Pluto's raw power will once again exert itself over women, since the Moon is close at hand here. Having Mercury conjunct Uranus, the Planet of Rebellion, means that

Is Leonardo DiCaprio a titanic actor or a heartbreaker extraordinaire?

Thanks to his Sun ✹, Mars ♏, and Venus ♐ all in Scorpio, Leo can act all right — on screen and off! There's a lot of power in this chart, so ladies had best beware.

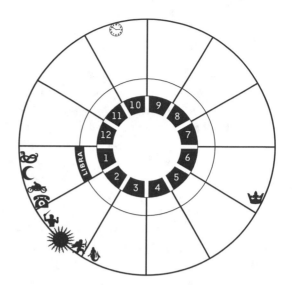

what Leo says often has a double meaning. Visiting the Planet of Communication here, Libra's vote is for tactful speech. Uranus, on the other hand, has the mental might to yield a progressive thinker with some radical ideas. Put the two together and Leonardo is having a ball with his clever wordplay.

It's Mars and Venus, both in Scorpio, which speak to DiCaprio's sexual leanings. With Venus, the Planet of Love, in Scorpio, look for a man who loves sex, plain and simple. Women will swoon over him thanks to his ever-present sexiness. Since Venus is conjunct DiCaprio's Scorpio Sun, a further emphasis is placed on the actor's charming good looks and pleasing persona. Women will find him sweetly irresistible and will respond to his feminine side. With Mars in Scorpio, DiCaprio's Planet of Energy is hypercharged and forceful, marking the actor as one who is driven, determined, and undeterred. This is one of the strongest placements that Mars can have and spells uncompromising courage and a will to overcome daunting odds. And yes, it speaks to sex appeal yet again.

A final look at DiCaprio's chart shows a Grand Water Trine in his celestial plan. This formation speaks to one who is good with emotions; intuition with career and money are also highlighted, since this placement falls into the Second, Sixth, and Tenth Houses. Expect DiCaprio to make smart choices for a long time to come.

Birth time source: "BCAA"

Julia Roberts

BORN: OCTOBER 28, 1967 12:16 AM SMYRNA, GEORGIA USA

The term "pretty woman" has truly found a home with Scorpio Julia Roberts. The Georgia Peach with the million-dollar smile was drawn to the stage early on, perhaps because she grew up alongside thespian sibs. Hitting the Big Apple in her late teens, Roberts played around with bit parts until she landed the role of irrepressible waitress in the film "Mystic Pizza." The actress's flowing mane and infectious giggle were hard to miss, and no one did. Roberts's next film, "Steel Magnolias," teamed her with a slew of Hollywood leading ladies and led to her much-ballyhooed turn as the hooker with a heart of gold (opposite Richard Gere this time) in the 1990 hit "Pretty Woman." Fame had its price, however, as the world soon became more obsessed with this looker's latest beau as opposed to her next role. Spending time with the likes of Liam Neeson, Daniel Day-Lewis, and Kiefer Sutherland did nothing to quash the chatter, and the actress's marriage and divorce to crooner Lyle Lovett created even more patter. Roberts's star turn in "My Best Friend's Wedding," however, has returned the focus to her roles.

Born with her Sun in Scorpio, Roberts is determined, sexy, and mysterious. This steel magnolia is steely, indeed, and possessed of the shrewd and penetrating demeanor which is the hallmark of the Scorpion. Passionate as well, Roberts will be motivated to reach her goals; conversely, the actress can be jealous and even unforgiving toward those who get in her way. With her Sun in the Fourth House of Home, much of Roberts's energy will be directed toward making her home feel safe and nurturing. As is the province of Scorpions, the very private Roberts will consider her home a sacred space and will strive to keep prying eyes well away.

It's her Moon in Leo which speaks to Roberts's fluid emotional state. Generally sunny in disposition, Roberts may spend a lot of time thinking about herself (Lions do love their throne) but will also be aware of the feelings of others. Since her Moon is in the Second House of Possessions, the actress will need to feel financially secure in order to be happy. ($17 million per film should buy plenty of happiness!) The actress's Moon is also square Neptune, the Planet of Make-Believe, which points toward some chaotic days. Roberts may find herself confused about her feelings and torn between fantasy and reality. Since Neptune is in the Fifth House of Romance, expect muddled emotions in affairs of the heart. Lastly, with her Moon making an out-of-sign conjunction to Jupiter, Roberts will be lucky with money and helpful to others. Since this conjunction is afflicted, however, our peach may be vulnerable to the emotional pleas of others.

With her Rising Sign in Cancer, this leading lady will be seen as sensitive, instinctive, and even introspective. The Crab on the Ascendant is the signal of one who is nurturing as well. It's Mercury, the Planet of Communication, in Scorpio which gives the actress her

What's behind Julia Roberts's sunny disposition?

It's a Leo Moon ☾ which casts a golden glow over this pretty woman's personality. Since her Moon makes an out-of-sign con-junction to Jupiter ♕, Roberts revels in helping others. What a gal!

love of investigation and disdain for glib speech. She yearns to go deep, probing issues with fervor and, hopefully, with others who share this trait.

Thanks to her Venus in Virgo, we now see why Roberts has a list of gorgeous exes. She's holding out for Mr. Right! No, make that Mr. Perfect, since the Virgin paired with the Planet of Love spells P-I-C-K-Y. Consequently, Roberts will keep playing the field until she hits the jackpot. Having Venus in Virgo is the cause of more conflicting energies in the heavens: beautiful Venus does not take easily to the Virgin's nit-picking, so love becomes one big effort for the discriminating Roberts. With Venus, Uranus, and Pluto all visiting the Virgin, a Virgo stellium is in evidence in the actress's chart. This stellium is the mark of the charismatic, one who can get her way with little more than a smile. Lucky Julia will have men at her feet, yet she'll be too persnickety to do anything about it!

Roberts's Mars, the Planet of Passion, in trusty Capricorn is the best indicator of her ambi-tion and resolve. Cap's role here is that of taskmaster, seeing to it that the actress puts in the hours required to get the job done. The job, in this case, is global domination, or at a minimum, real success. With her Mars square Saturn in Aries, however, Roberts's bold-ness is restrained. The actress may lack confidence and fear defeat at critical moments.

A final look at Roberts's chart shows all her planets except Saturn below the horizon. Read: an extremely private person who is hiding from the world, much like her planets.

Birth time source: Lois Rodden

Meg Ryan

BORN: NOVEMBER 19, 1961 10:36 AM FAIRFIELD, CONNECTICUT USA

Perky. Bouncy. Bubbly. Is this the curse of every blue-eyed blonde? Perhaps, but these words are on the mark when the blonde in question is Scorpion Meg Ryan. The former homecoming queen may have headed off to college to study journalism, but she quickly found herself bitten by the acting bug. Her early credits were on the soaps, the kind of over-the-top acting which no doubt helped her achieve a wonderful (albeit faked) orgasm in "When Harry Met Sally." "Sleepless in Seattle," a sentimental turn with actor Tom Hanks, followed and established Ryan as a romantic comedy star. While favoring lighter roles, Ryan has earned her dramatic stripes as an alcoholic wife in "When a Man Loves a Woman" and as a wartime pilot in "Courage Under Fire." Married to actor Dennis Quaid, Ryan sees no need to mess with success: "You've Got Mail" reunites her with Hanks in a tale of high-tech romance.

Born with her Sun in Scorpio, Ryan is intense, penetrating, and resourceful. Make no mistake, this is a woman who knows what she wants and knows how to get it. The flip side of the Scorpionic personality is an individual who is secretive, suspicious, and prone to steamrolling the competition. As one of the power Signs of the Zodiac, Scorpions are not to be taken lightly. Where Ryan is concerned, clearly she is much more than meets the eye. The core qualities of the Scorpio-born are determination and strength of purpose coupled with the strongest of wills. These folks fear no one and nothing and are content to forge ahead in their quest to conquer the highest of mountains. Never will a Scorpion pretend to agree simply to keep the peace.

With her Moon in Aries, Ryan is a woman in a hurry. The actress wants things, and she wants them now; this quality makes it no surprise that her successes came early. Along with this comes a quick temper and some strong opinions. An Aries Moon also speaks to a competitive childhood and rejection by the mother. The actress has her Mercury (Communication Planet), Venus (Love Planet), and Neptune (the Planet of Fantasy and Make-Believe) all in Scorpio and positioned closely together in the heavens. This alignment intensifies Ryan's Scorpionic qualities, and the introduction of Neptune indicates that Ryan can make you believe whatever she wants. Is she really as effusive and happy-go-lucky as she appears? Perhaps, perhaps not.

Ryan's Rising Sign is Capricorn, leading her to present herself to the world as an ambitious individual who won't be denied. Since Capricorn is ruled by Saturn, the Planet of Discipline and Hard Work, it's a safe bet that Harry's "Sally" is hardest on herself despite any appearances to the contrary. This serious-minded, hardworking attitude is supported by the rest of Ryan's chart. The actress is also likely to get better with age, which means we can expect to see more of her in the years to come.

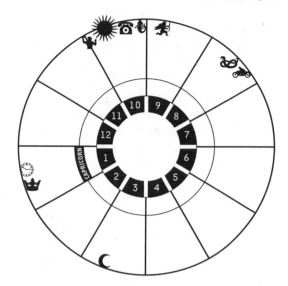

Is the real Meg Ryan as perky as she appears?

Ryan has her Sun ☀, Venus 🐗, and Mercury ☎ all in secretive Scorpio. Oh, and Neptune, too, which means that she can be a chameleon if she chooses. Will the real Meg please stand up?

Looking at the relationships between the planets in Ryan's chart, one finds Saturn making a square, or hard angle, to her Aries Moon. This would indicate that the actress is reluctant to let her true feelings out, leading to a suppressed, even repressed persona. Ryan feels a need to be the good soldier, offering the world the picture which is most agreeable. This square in Ryan's chart speaks to a real actress and a trouper who may well be shouldering some heavy burdens. Even so, the heavy Scorpio influence in this chart shows us someone who is very sexual, the hunter in a romantic relationship. Scorpions may be mysterious and hard to predict, but they also sizzle between the sheets!

Ryan also has a number of planets in the Tenth House, the Sector of Vocation and Social Status. Reputation can be everything to these folks, which may explain why Ryan is keen on her smiling, fresh-faced persona. Those who exhibit this planetary grouping share a mantra along the lines of "I will be at the top and nothing will get in my way!" Look out, world, Meg just may.

Birth time source: Steinbercher

Winona Ryder

BORN: OCTOBER 29, 1971 11:00 AM WINONA, MINNESOTA USA

Behind the pixie-ish haircut and the big brown eyes beats the heart of a young woman who is a standard-bearer for the Gen X crowd she represents. Scorpion Winona Ryder is an actress with both spunk and soul, and she certainly showed plenty of the former in her career-launching role as the classmate-from-hell in the black comedy "Heathers." Quirky roles in "Edward Scissorhands" (with then-beau Johnny Depp) and "Night on Earth" followed, leading to more subdued period pieces like "The Age of Innocence" and "Little Women." Our Winona may look like the girl next door, but she's somehow managed to lay waste to a succession of suitors: Johnny Depp, Christian Slater, Daniel Day-Lewis, and David Duchovny can all lay claim to the title of "Winona's ex." And how about studly Matt Damon? This daughter of hippie intellectuals (and goddaughter of the late LSD lord Timothy Leary) is bound to keep him guessing!

Born with her Sun in Scorpio, Ryder is mysterious and secretive. This is a young woman who knows how to command attention, and when she sets her mind to something, that's it. As is the case with those born under a Scorpio Sun, Ryder is motivated, passionate, and ultra-determined. Since her Moon is in Pisces, the actress is a very emotional person who easily picks up on the feelings of others. Her brand of acting is no doubt experiential, as she uses her sharp instincts and gut feelings to lead the way. Ryder's Moon also pegs her as a compassionate soul, someone who is happy to help those in need. With both her Sun (Scorpio) and Moon (Pisces) being Water Signs, Johnny's ex is both highly emotional and intuitive. If you think those big brown eyes are looking right through you, they are! Ryder may look like sweetness and light, but rest assured there's a lot going on underneath.

With her Rising Sign in Sagittarius, Ryder's persona to the world is the one of the ever-popular jokester. She will appear light-hearted and easy-going, although this isn't the sum of things. As the bachelorette Sign of the Zodiac, those graced with Sagittarius in their charts are notoriously hard to pin down, because relationships are multi-layered for them. Remember, Sagittarius is also the Sign of the philosopher, so things tend to run deep here. While Ryder's outer manner may appear friendly and outgoing and she may well demonstrate a charming curiosity about others, she is quite intense when she takes a relationship to the next level. Superficial guys need not apply! That said, the actress knows how to keep a sense of humor about things, even falling prey to the occasional bout of foot-in-mouth.

Ryder's Mercury and Venus are both in Scorpio, which means that her Communication and Love Planets, respectively, are right next to each other in the heavens. Back on Earth, this magnifies the actress's intensity in love relationships. Make no mistake, once Ryder

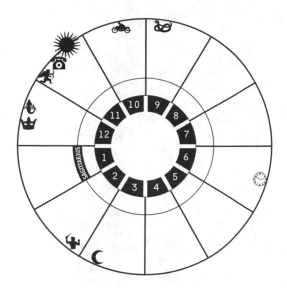

Why is Winona Ryder such an original?

With her Mars ♒ in Aquarius, this free-thinking, independent woman has a flair for innovation and plenty of original thought.

sets her eyes on someone, it's over. Hmmm, make that just beginning, for this lady will not be denied! Ryder knows how to make a connection: she is a charming conversationalist who knows exactly when to probe further. Words do not fail her, and she always manages to say the right thing. Having her Mercury and Venus in Scorpio emphasizes her Scorpio Sun, enhancing her gift of persuasion — and she's shrewd to boot. It's unlikely that any man she desires will have the word "no" in his vocabulary.

Thanks to her Mars in Aquarius, the actress's Passion Planet gives her considerable drive, energy, and a flair for innovation. She is definitely an original. Those influenced by Aquarius are also independent and free thinkers, qualities akin to her parents' sensibilities. Although Ryder's Sagittarius Rising also creates a love of freedom, this is tempered by a very Scorpionic neediness. The actress will often be torn by a desire to be her own woman while at the same time craving the emotional comfort of another.

With more planets in the Eastern part of the sky at her time of birth, Ryder is an initiator, one who will create her own destiny. She's not keen on taking orders and will be much happier when setting her own boundaries. With no Earth Signs (Taurus, Virgo, Capricorn) in her chart, Ryder can be a bit impractical and devoid of materialistic tendencies. For this reason, an Earth Sign would be a most suitable match for this formidable young woman.

Birth time source: Steinbercher

Other famous Scorpions:

Prince Charles
Hillary Clinton
Danny DeVito
Sally Field
Calista Flockhart
Jodie Foster
Bill Gates
Whoopi Goldberg
Ethan Hawke
Goldie Hawn
Lauren Holly
Jenny McCarthy
Matthew McConaughey
Dylan McDermott
Demi Moore
Joaquin Phoenix
Roseanne
David Schwimmer
Martin Scorsese
Sam Shepard

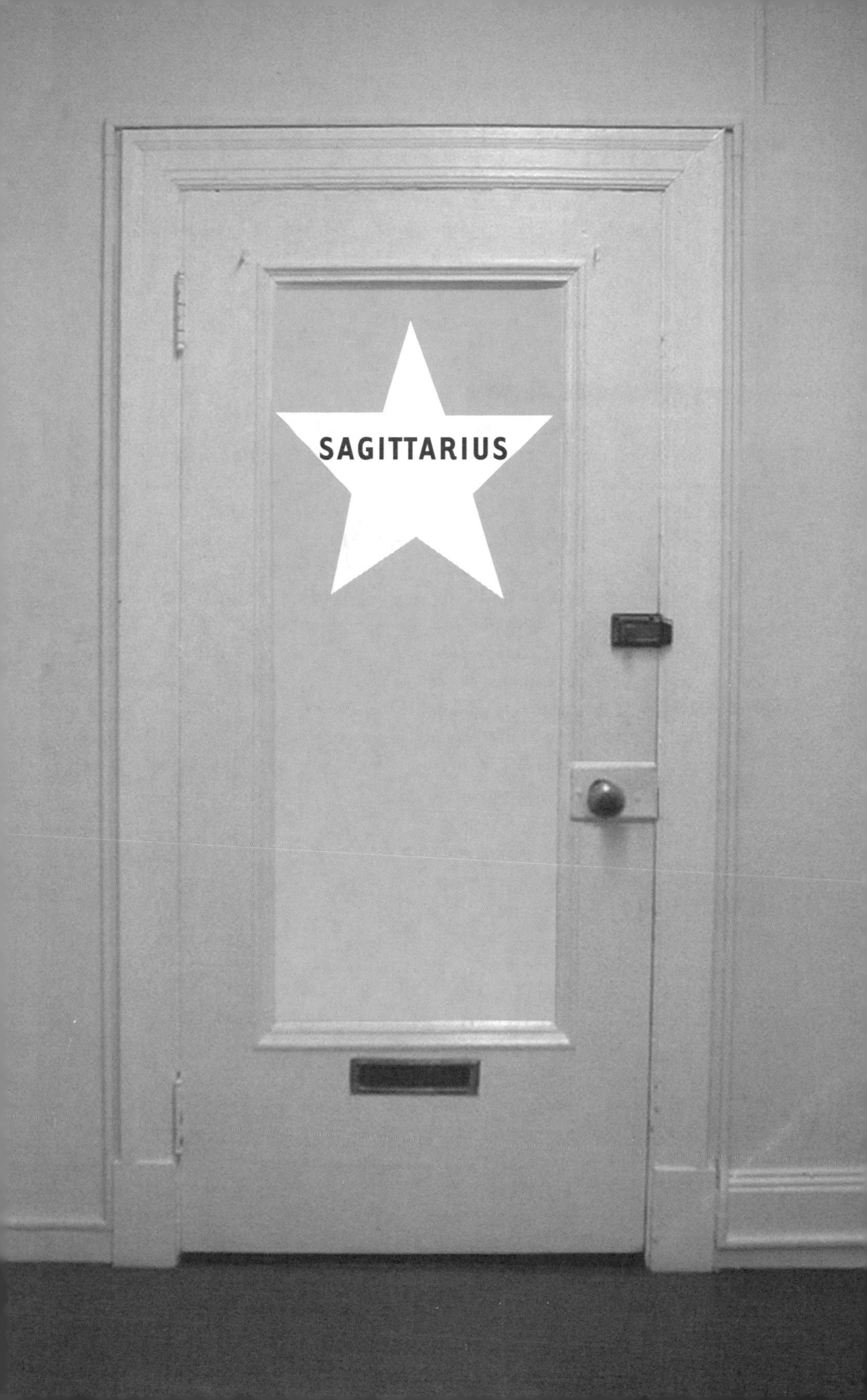
SAGITTARIUS

Sagittarius: The Archer

That little kid who hits the road with a knapsack over his shoulder is the prototypical Sagittarian. Those born under this Sign are the adventurers of the Zodiac, eager to explore, gain knowledge, and learn the truth. See, Sags are all about the truth, as if the world were some big lie. These folks read, ask questions, make visits, and then question some more — all to satisfy their quest for the truth and, more importantly, the meaning of life. Heavy burdens, but the Archer is happy to shoulder them. After all, this Archer is a Centaur, half man, half beast, and all muscle. And when the Archer flings those arrows, you can bet his aim is true.

Sagittarius rules the Ninth House, the House of Philosophy. Sags are keenly interested in the "why" of life and are forever thinking of ways to get the answers they need. They'll read books, attend workshops, explore various religions and cultures — anything that might expand their base of knowledge and give them the comfort they seek. As a result, it's not uncommon to find Sags as scholars and professors, immersed in university life. A traveling professorship is best, however, since these folks do love to span the globe. Sags need their freedom more than most any other Sign, so they've got to get out there and interact with their clan. This urge for freedom and continual learning is in keeping with the Mutable Quality which is assigned to this Sign. The Sag's desire to move, learn, and probe can prove intriguing to others so long as these folks don't get carried away with themselves. The Archer is a pretty self-assured beast and can appear impulsive, aggressive, and even hot-headed on occasion. Brushing up on "How to Win Friends and Influence People" is good advice for a Sagittarian.

Being ruled by the Planet Jupiter, the Planet of Expansion, means that Sags should be aware of their propensity to get:
1. Big-headed
2. Big-mouthed

Here's why:
1. They almost always think they're right
2. They love to exaggerate

Big for Sagittarians also refers to big minds, so those born under this Sign have an appetite for knowledge which is unrivaled. They love to explore theories and possibilities, a quality in keeping with their philosophical nature. Jupiter is also known as the Planet of Luck, which means that these folks could hit it big at the gaming tables. Leave it to a Sag to discover the best way to beat the house! While charming and adaptable in most situations, Sagittarians can also appear self-indulgent and a bit caught up with themselves. With any kind of luck, though, they'll soon focus their energies on a new course of study and concentrate on that.

The Element associated with Sagittarius is Fire, which should come as no surprise. These folks are action-oriented, hitting the road in search of adventure, knowledge, and understanding. They are freedom-loving and broad-minded, qualities which may make them a bit too restless for home life. Face it, these folks are considered the bachelors of the Zodiac for a reason. It's that combustible Sag personality which lends itself much better to cocktail parties than to quiet evenings at home. Like a quick-moving fire, Sags can get things going but might fan off in several different directions before completing anything. No problem, since they will have picked up lots of good information along the way.

Sagittarians are no shrinking violets. Quite the opposite, they are often the life of the party, amusing a group with tales of their adventures and spiffy witticisms. These folks are funny, outgoing, and fun-loving. They also love to flirt, so get ready! Sagittarians can easily find themselves in love with three people at the same time. Explaining this situation to the parties involved, however, may prove somewhat more challenging. At times like this, a Sag might want to call in a referee, since they themselves tend to be a bit too blunt for their own good. "What's wrong with my approach?" the optimistic, idealistic Sag will wail. "Everybody's happy, right?" Yeah, right.

The field of play (that other field) is one where the Sag prefers to go it alone. Sports to the Archer are yet another challenge of strength and will, so think extreme sports. Play can also take in some mental gymnastics, such as chess or a game of high-stakes poker. More engaging play is a spirited debate, and you can bet (please do) that a Sag will never back down from their position. Since Sagittarians are prone to hip and thigh problems, they should hope to never have to run for their lives.

The Sagittarius-born are knowledge-driven, philosophical souls who live for their search for the truth. They prefer to span the globe in search of answers, collecting adventures (and playmates) along the way. If they stay at home long enough, invite them over to your next party!

Kim Basinger
BORN: DECEMBER 8, 1953 ATHENS, GEORGIA USA

Cover-girl looks are what got Sagittarian Kim Basinger noticed in the first place, a look which proceeded to be plastered on magazine covers for over a decade. While modeling proved lucrative for Basinger, the comely blonde really wanted to act. Switching coasts (New York to L.A.), fame finally came after "9 1/2 Weeks." This psycho-sexual drama, alongside Mickey Rourke, catapulted Basinger into the big leagues. Although heating up the screen in films such as "Batman" made for more good notices, most of the ink on the actress covered her off-screen exploits. Playing with the Artist (while he was still Prince) proved juicy enough, but Basinger managed to top that by buying her own town — Braselton, Georgia. Sadly, she had to give it back (sell it, to be exact) as part of a fiasco involving a sour movie deal. Basinger rebounded nicely, however, by marrying her co-star in "The Marrying Man," the equally good-looking Alec Baldwin. Her Oscar for "L.A. Confidential" and the birth of daughter Ireland were merely icing on a very rich cake!

Born with her Sun in Sagittarius, Basinger is a straightforward and broad-minded woman with a generous spirit. Philosophically inclined, the actress is likely to focus on higher ideals, seek spiritual comfort, and embrace a sense of fair play. The optimistic Archer will fling its arrows to the consternation of none, since the Sag-born are popular, free-spirited, and even daring at times. That said, a Sag in a snit can be pushy, self-indulgent, and woefully short on tact. With her Sun opposite Jupiter, look for Basinger to overestimate her abilities while underestimating her competition. Is there ego at play here? You bet. Her dogma will rule, whether it's on behalf of PETA (a favorite animal cause) or the trusty Democrats.

It's her Moon in Capricorn which gives this Bat gal her cool demeanor. That icy turn in "L.A. Confidential" was no act. Basinger can switch her feelings on and off and is often aloof. Cap's emotional blanket has security written all over it, too, so expect Basinger to feel best when her family and finances are in solid shape. Privacy is very important to the actress as well; while she needs to be needed, it's Basinger herself who makes it tough for those she loves to get really close to her.

With Mercury in Scorpio, the actress is firm in her beliefs and presents them with considerable zeal. Changing this woman's mind is a ridiculous proposition, since the Scorpion won't have it. A better strategy would be to engage Basinger in chatter that matters, although her gift for strategy will surely win the day. Since Mercury is square Pluto, the Planet of Raw Power, here, Basinger is a very suspicious woman. She'll formulate her plans in secret and be forever on the lookout for spies. Further, not only is the actress opinionated, she won't hesitate to force her opinions on others.

Why is a sense of fair play important to Kim Basinger?

Thanks to her Sun ☀ in Sagittarius, the actress's lofty ideals are always on an even keel. With her Venus 🏹 in Sag as well, love is also fair game for Basinger. And who better to take her heart than a Libran whose Scales yearn for balance?

Thanks to Venus in Sagittarius, the Archer's arrows are now flung in the name of love. Love for Basinger is all about possibilities, although the mating dance will be of no use to this lady if it inhibits her freedom. Sag in the Planet of Love also speaks to an idealistic and adventurous love, so Basinger will want to keep things fluid and interesting. As if that wasn't enough, the babe in Basinger is utterly flirtatious. With Mercury making an out-of-sign conjunction to Venus in the heavens, the beautiful Basinger will always look good and manage to say the right thing to both friends and lovers.

Basinger's Mars in Libra looks pretty good, too, since the Planet of Passion is polished to a sheen by lovely Libra. Partnership is emphasized here, so expect the actress to accomplish more as a team than solo. She'll also need the approval of others to keep her going. With her Mars conjunct Neptune, Basinger may be prone to hiding a few things. Conversely, Neptune's energy allows this lady to put her dreams front and center while Mars moves them forward (her beloved animals stand one heck of a chance!). Both Mars and Neptune are square Uranus, the Planet of Rebellion, in Basinger's chart, not a good sign. While Mars's square to Uranus speaks to an impatient thrill-seeker who is willful and possibly reckless, Neptune's square to Uranus points to a scorched earth policy. Playing along with this lady may be your best bet.

Birth time source: not available. As a result, references to the Rising Sign, Moon, and Houses may be omitted from this profile.

Bette Midler

BORN: DECEMBER 1, 1945 2:19 PM HONOLULU, HAWAII USA

She's a sassy, brassy, big-talkin', big-hearted gal who can make her presence known in no time flat. No wonder they call Sagittarian Bette Midler "The Divine Miss M!" This dynamo is a pro at self-deprecating humor, something which has helped endear her to everyone from young girls to housewives and the gay men for whom she started out singing in New York City's bathhouses. Taking her lusty pipes to the silver screen, she sang up a storm in "The Rose," her first starring role. Since then, audiences have enjoyed her bravado in films such as "Down and Out in Beverly Hills" and "Ruthless People." Her performance alongside fellow classy gals Goldie Hawn and Diane Keaton in "The First Wives Club" spoke to every middle-aged woman with a yearning for vengeance. No thoughts of revenge for the Divine Miss M, however, as she and hubby Martin Von Haselberg both enjoy doting on daughter Sophie. With "Bathhouse Betty," a chart climber, what will Bette do for an encore?

Born with her Sun in Sagittarius, Midler is a funny and straightforward woman who can see the humor in most any situation. Sagittarians are the probers of the Zodiac, and they will be happy to engage you in conversation for hours. The hope is that it won't deteriorate into an argument, since these folks can be rather blunt and even pushy where their agenda is concerned. That said, the Sag in Midler makes her a fairly broadminded person, one who is open to most people and situations. She is also generous in spirit, enthusiastic, and talkative to the point of exaggeration. This freedom-loving gal can also be self-indulgent, and when you're as fabulous as Bette, why not?

With her Moon in Scorpio, Midler's emotions tend toward the passionate side of things. The Divine One can be probing and secretive, yet these traits have a nice shiny patina on them. She may be nailing you to the wall, but you won't even know it! As a result of the Scorpionic flow, Midler is also motivated and determined, and certainly someone to be reckoned with. She is also keenly perceptive. It's a Rising Sign in Aries that gives Midler her patented spunk and bluntness. Her image to the world, as dictated by her Rising Sign, is one of a woman in a hurry. Don't get in her way! She's got places to go, people to see, and things to do. With the combination of Aries Rising and a Sagittarius Sun, Midler is pegged as a true pioneer, one who is happy to blaze the trail for others to come.

Thanks to her Venus in Scorpio, Midler is passionate and deep where her relationships are concerned. The actress's Love Planet marks her as someone who is intense and fiercely loyal to her lover. With Midler's Moon and Venus both in a feminine Sign (in this case Scorpio), her feminine side is very important to her as well. She will be devoted and protective of those she loves and will place great importance on personal relationships. Midler's Mercury, the Planet of Communication, is in Sagittarius, which emphasizes her

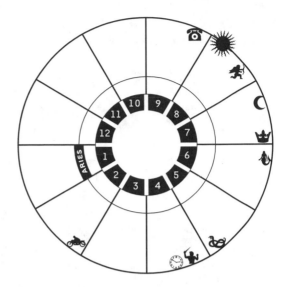

Why can Bette Midler see the humor in most any situation?

It's a Sagittarius Sun ☀ which tickles Midler's funny bone. With chatty Mercury ☎ in Sag, too, this lady's words are a hoot.

gift of gab. This woman is funny, quick, and wonderfully spontaneous. It's easy for her to speak on the fly, although at times she may come across as a bit unrefined, a trait which is supported by the Scorpio in her chart. As Scorpio is the Sign of Sex, it's not unusual for those influenced by this Sign to talk down and dirty. It's Mars in Leo, however, that makes Midler the dynamo she is. In her chart, the Planet of Passion is teamed up with the Sign known for drive and ambition. Look out, world! This is one proud, hardworking woman who will get herself to the top, all the while in full control.

Looking further at Midler's chart, she has a number of Fire planets (Aries, Leo, Sagittarius) in the heavens, contributing to her quick-moving, fiery persona. This woman jumps right in, with little thought to the potential downside of a situation. The lack of Earth planets in her chart adds to the likelihood that Midler's successes have been the result of sheer will and determination, as opposed to a plodding sensibility. With her Scorpio Moon making a square, or hard angle, to Pluto, the Planet of Power, the songstress is further pegged as a combustible woman possessed of the ruthless energy necessary to get ahead. Lastly, with most of her planets on the western side of the sky at the time of her birth, Midler is concerned with how others see her and craves approval. Lucky for her, she's getting plenty of that!

Birth time source: Gauquelin

Brad Pitt

BORN: DECEMBER 18, 1963 SHAWNEE, OKLAHOMA USA

Maybe they do grow 'em better in Oklahoma, or at least that's the conclusion one can draw from the looks of gorgeous Sagittarian Brad Pitt. Despite his protestations of wanting to be seen as a serious actor first and foremost, the onetime Sexiest Man Alive would be wise to come to grips with his killer good looks. Eager to try his luck in L.A., Pitt stumbled around Tinseltown until he landed a small but juicy role in 1991's "Thelma and Louise." Trading on his sex appeal (hey, he was poured into his jeans), the actor made Geena Davis's day and put a smile on many a female face. Pitt followed this up with the ensemble pieces "Legends of the Fall" and "Interview With the Vampire" and took the lead in "Seven," where he met his girl with "class," Gwyneth Paltrow. Although the romance went downhill (as did his trysts with actresses Robin Givens and Juliette Lewis), Pitt's work was on a decidedly upward spiral. His performances in "12 Monkeys" and "Seven Years in Tibet" earned the actor much-sought-after praise. Ahhh, to be taken seriously!

Born with his Sun in Sagittarius, Pitt is a straight-ahead sort with a generous spirit, and he loves his freedom. In keeping with the Archer's whim, Pitt is philosophically-inclined and an avid seeker of the truth. That role in "Seven Years in Tibet" clearly spoke to the actor's sensibilities. Generally optimistic in nature, Sags can be argumentative on occasion and are prone to procrastination. Somehow, waiting for Brad doesn't sound like a bad thing! Since Sag is the bachelor Sign of the Zodiac, however, patient lady friends may come to realize that they'll be waiting for a long time.

With his Mercury in Capricorn, expect Pitt's speech to be of the serious and well-thought-out variety. The actor is disciplined mentally thanks to the Goat and also has the ability to concentrate when needed. Common sense is the Brad man's ruler, not sheer intellect. Since his Mercury is conjunct Venus, Pitt is unlikely to stick his foot in his mouth. Quite the contrary: his patter will be gracious, friendly, and especially appealing to women. With his Mercury conjunct Mars, however, the actor can be quite determined in a verbal joust. Pitt's Mercury is also trine Uranus and Pluto in the heavens, good aspects for him. It's Mercury trine Uranus which marks Pitt as a clever, original thinker who is never at a loss for words, while Mercury's trine to Pluto speaks to a shrewd fellow who plans well (a quality supported by Capricorn). Bottom line: Pitt has a plan and is executing it, so the payoff should be his.

Thanks to Venus in Capricorn as well, Pitt likes the idea of a trophy woman on his arm. Even so, he'll be conservative in the game of love, preferring a merger for the sake of practicality and status as opposed to a passion-filled dalliance. Pitt may gravitate toward an older, more-established partner since love, as prophesied by the Goat, is often just another business proposition.

Brad Pitt isn't just another pretty face — or is he?

With Mercury  in Capricorn trine both Uranus 🏍 and Pluto ♇, the actor has a plan and is executing it to perfection. Bottom line: Pitt is definitely substance over style! But even serious boys like to play, so look for an Aquarian in Pitt's sandbox.

It's Mars in Capricorn (yet again) in Pitt's celestial spec which drives the actor toward his goals. There's a lot of ambition in this man's makeup, so expect him to be well-organized and industrious as a result. Since his Mars is square Jupiter in Aries, Pitt is plenty competitive, to the point of fearlessness. The actor will take risks with his career and won't shy away from a fight. Thanks to lucky Jupiter, he'll probably roll sevens every time. Pitt's Mars is also trine Uranus and Pluto, both very favorable aspects. Mars trine Uranus marks Pitt as innovative, a bit unconventional, and certainly daring (think extreme sports here) while Mars's trine to Pluto is the sign of one who is courageous and doesn't know defeat. These latter aspects possess the kind of charismatic energy which defines Pitt.

Looking at the actor's chart a bit further, we see Jupiter in Aries, the sign of one who believes in himself. "I can do this!" Pitt will exclaim, and he knows it for a fact. Further, the actor is happy to back his bravado with action and panache. Lastly, Pitt's Saturn is in Aquarius, the mark of a rational, sometimes detached man. Since Saturn is squaring Neptune, the Planet of Illusion, here, expect Pitt to seek validation for his talent and hard work and not as just another pretty face .

Birth time source: not available. As a result, references to the Rising Sign, Moon, and Houses may be omitted from this profile.

Steven Spielberg
BORN: DECEMBER 18, 1946 6:16 PM CINCINNATI, OHIO USA

Doing a Top Ten List of Sagittarian Steven Spielberg's movies would be a daunting task. Where to start? Well, the director himself started awfully young, making his first movie at the age of twelve and staging a premiere of his first feature film at the age of sixteen. He hit pay dirt with an early TV flick, "Duel," a taut thriller pitting Dennis Weaver against a wayward eighteen-wheeler, helped launch his storied career. "Jaws," "Close Encounters of the Third Kind," and then "Raiders of The Lost Ark" with pal George Lucas all led to Spielberg's most beloved film, "E.T.," a touching tale of a little boy and his magical friend which speaks volumes about the director's sense of wonder and imagination. A more sober turn as producer/director defined Spielberg's career : "Schindler's List," the story of one man's attempt to save Jews during World War II, finally earned Spielberg the Oscars he so richly deserved. Married to actress Kate Capshaw, the mind behind DreamWorks continues to dream big.

Born with his Sun in Sagittarius, Spielberg is an enthusiastic man who is driven to understand his world and find the truth in it. As the Sign of the philosopher, Sagittarians want to probe, explore, and get answers. They are also optimistic, independent, and love their freedom. Shooting on location is a natural for this director, as he loves a change of scenery and the opportunity to learn from other cultures. Face it, Indy Jones wasn't a far cry from his creator! With a Sagittarius Sun, expect Spielberg to be focused on religious and spiritual matters as well. Sagittarians may not be great at commitment (this is the bachelor Sign of the Zodiac), but they are exceedingly idealistic.

It's Spielberg's Moon in Scorpio which channels all of his great ideas and gives them shape. As the keeper of his emotions, the director's Moon marks him as intense, emotional, and very driven. He is passionate about what he believes in (a quality reinforced by his Sag Sun) and possesses great resolve. This can make for some combustible outtakes, but that's life. Bottom line: when the director sets his mind to something, that's it. Cut. End of story.

With a Rising Sign of Cancer, Spielberg's picture to the world is one of a family man who is both protective and nurturing. Think E.T.'s Dad. The director will also be focused on traditions and the past, which explains his devotion to his own Shoah Foundation, an organization that record the stories of those affected by the Holocaust. The Crab's influence also speaks to a good memory and a keen instinct. It's Mercury in Sagittarius as well, which allows Spielberg to give voice to his ideas. He may occasionally speak before he thinks, but he'll always be ready to talk about his ideas. And expect this man to go deep, since Sag visiting Mercury is the mark of the prober, one who will know a great deal

Why is Steven Spielberg so passionate and idealistic?

The director's Sag Sun ☀ is visionary and full of ideas; his Scorpio Moon ☾ fervently pleads the case. This one-two punch is hard to beat!

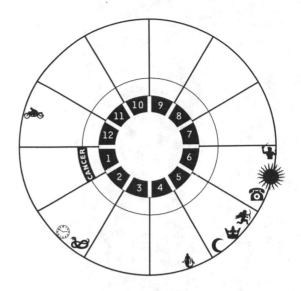

about the things that he considers important. Along these lines, this principled thinker will place a premium on freedom of speech.

Thanks to his Venus in Scorpio, Spielberg has the charm and magnetism to maintain his public standing. With his Planet of Love in the House of Romance — wow! Spielberg will certainly sizzle in the love department, exhibiting passion and considerable sex appeal. He'll shrewdly focus in on the object of his affections and bam! It's done. Further, his Venus comes together with Jupiter, the Planet of Luck and Good Fortune, in Scorpio as well. This tells us that personal happiness and luck will probably follow this man around. Expect Spielberg to be well-liked by his peers and to enjoy the camaraderie and goodwill that this receptive energy brings. This alignment also signals an aesthete moved by all things beautiful. Fortunate in love, lucky in money — this is no dream in the works, it's Spielberg's reality.

Mars, the Planet of Passion, is visiting Capricorn in Spielberg's chart, which helps explain how he's gotten to where he's at. This placement gives the director ambition and determination. The ideals of Sagittarius are shaped by Capricorn and molded into something that works. Spielberg seeks recognition and prestige and will continue to work until he believes that it's his. And then he'll work for more, since it's unlikely that he'll retire. With more planets in fixed Signs (Taurus, Leo, Scorpio, Aquarius) than not, Spielberg will never give up.

Birth time source: Lois Rodden

Other famous
Sagittarians:

Woody Allen
Christina Applegate
Tyra Banks
Kenneth Branagh
Jeff Bridges
Jamie Lee Curtis
Jane Fonda
Daryl Hannah
Ed Harris
Teri Hatcher
Samuel L. Jackson
Don Johnson
John F. Kennedy, Jr.
John Malkovich
Alyssa Milano
Keith Richards
Ben Stiller
Kiefer Sutherland
Marisa Tomei
Tina Turner

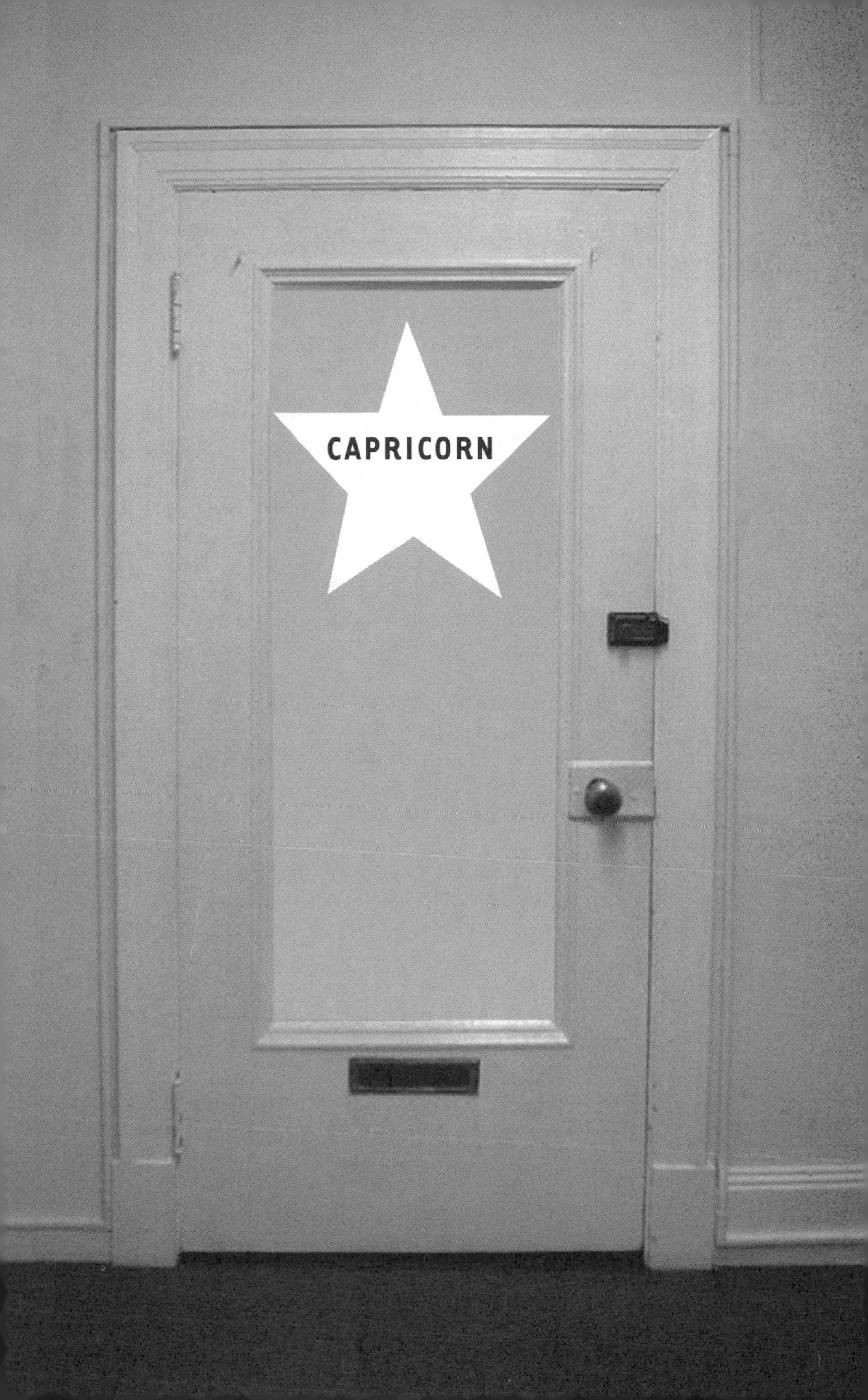
CAPRICORN

Capricorn: The Goat

Donald Trump may not be a Capricorn, but he sure acts like one. Those born under this Sign are ambitious, hard working, and determined to succeed — and they love the spoils which success brings. It's not like The Donald goes out for a burger 'n fries, y'know. Expect to see Capricorns at fund-raising dinners and society events, the better to let the world know that they've arrived. Their favorite causes are likely to be in keeping with their traditional bent, and while they won't be loudly dressed, you'll surely notice them thanks to their quiet yet self-assured dignity. You can bet that any Capricorns who haven't arrived just yet are working hard to get there.

Capricorn rules the Tenth House, the House of Social Status. This Sign's alter ego, the Goat, has one aim in life: to climb to the top of the mountain. You think it's any fun wallowing in the valley? Sheesh, it's full of mosquitoes down there. On the other hand, the air is pure and clean at the top, and it smells of success. So the Goat will climb a few steps every day, slowly but steadily making its way to the top. Capricorns will succeed because they are ambitious and dedicated to achieving their goals. Working in their favor is a practical, realistic temperament and single-mindedness of purpose which allows them to keep their eyes on the prize. Capricorns are adept at starting businesses and are full of ideas, which is to be expected when you consider the Cardinal nature of this Sign. These folks are initiators but are also sensible about what they undertake. They tend toward the conservative, a quality which may make them overly cautious on occasion. Even so, their organizational skills and persistence allow them to forge ahead.

When you are ruled by Saturn, the Planet of Discipline and Responsibility, don't expect to go around smiling all the time. Such is the lot of Capricorns. Luckily for these folks, they enjoy hard work, so even if they're not smiling outwardly, they are cheering themselves along inside with every success. Anyway, since the successful get invited to fancy dinners and parties, the Cap will surely get the last laugh. All of the Goat's hard work is for a reason: to be accepted and to gain the social status which comes with it. Appearances are important to Capricorns, and when they do get their moment in the sun, expect these folks to handle it with grace and poise. Those born under this Sign can be reserved to the point of inhibition, but they'd much rather appear self-controlled than glib.

Since the Element associated with Capricorn is Earth, expect a grounded and practical sort who enjoys putting in a good day's work. Capricorns are the worker bees of the Zodiac, making them highly industrious and, as a result, intolerant of the weaknesses of others. The Goat understands one and only one thing: work. Capricorns set high standards for themselves and others and expect them to be met. They can be worriers, too,

concerned that their best efforts (which are considerable) won't be enough. For this reason, Caps can be thrifty, living in fear of the proverbial rainy day. With this individual's
work ethic, however, the raindrops rarely come. At times, the Cap will spend frivolously,
thinking that a nice shiny car, for example, might impress the neighbors. Or maybe, it's
just that these folks are prepping for their big payday!

Fun activities for the Goat include:
1. Counting (their money)
2. Working (overtime)
3. Climbing (to the top)

Capricorns tend to be conventional and responsible folks. They don't want to make a big
splash, they just want to reach their goals and attain a measure of success. If that con-
fers with it some power and prestige, hey, why not? Being at the top is bound to catch
someone's eye, which is how Goats often hitch up. Those born under this Sign tend to be
too busy working to find that special someone. However, if that person finds them, well,
great! Capricorns aren't likely to be hearts and flowers types, though. It's much more
likely that they'll show their love by providing a comfortable home and a safe and stable
environment. The Goat is loyal, devoted, and not likely to stray from their mate, which
may explain why Donald Trump is not a Capricorn.

When it comes to sports and recreation, Capricorns like a lively game of anything. Since
these folks are good at getting to the finish line, be sure to have them on your team.
Everyone had better be prepared to play, too, since Caps loathe a slacker. In the physical
body, Capricorn rules the knees, teeth, and bones, so kneepads and a mask are de
rigueur. Maybe even full-body armor.

The Capricorn-born are tireless workers who know how to set goals and achieve them. All
this work is for a reason: these folks love the trappings of success and wouldn't mind seeing their name in the financial press. To the victor go the spoils!

Nicolas Cage

BORN: JANUARY 7, 1964 5:35 AM HARBOR CITY, CALIFORNIA USA

Growing up, Capricorn Nicolas Cage spent summers at his uncle Francis's house in San Francisco. Luckily for this budding actor, his uncle is Francis Ford Coppola, which no doubt led to some pretty spiffy lessons. Determined to make it on his own, however, young Nic soon changed his surname to Cage after a favorite comic-book hero. It wasn't long before the actor started landing screen roles opposite leading ladies, working with Kathleen Turner in "Peggy Sue Got Married," Holly Hunter in "Raising Arizona," and Cher in her Oscar-winning turn in "Moonstruck." Cage earned an Oscar of his own for his gritty performance as the down-on-life drunk in "Leaving Las Vegas." A slew of action flicks showcasing a buffed-up Cage followed, most notably "The Rock" and "Con Air." Married to actress Patricia Arquette, it's Cage's blend of he-man and everyman qualities (along with the ethereal in "City Of Angels") which makes him particularly appealing.

Born with his Sun in Capricorn, Cage is ambitious and determined and possessed of the discipline that will take him to where he wants to go. Capricorn is the Sign of the hard working, and these people will usually achieve great things in their chosen field. Rest assured that the actor is just warming up! When things aren't going their way, however, they can become cold, calculating, and rather rigid. Even so, it's unlikely that Cage will take his eye off his intended prize: fame, fortune, and the respect of his peers.

It's Cage's Moon in Libra which gives the actor his particular brand of appeal. This place-ment, dealing with emotions as it does, marks Cage as a charming and sociable fellow, someone who won't fly off the handle and will keep the peace at all costs. Face it, this is one cool customer! With a Rising Sign of Sagittarius, Cage's friendly and cheerful persona is reinforced. What we see in Cage is an outgoing, open-minded individual who may on occasion speak before he thinks. In Cage's case, it's important to note that this is what we see — the Capricorn in his chart pegs him as more serious than he appears. This Sagittarian influence also tells us that Cage is curious on a broad scale and would enjoy getting to know people from other countries and cultures. This is someone who wants to learn from experience as opposed to theory. Further, he is also an optimist and couples that enthusiasm for life with a good sense of humor.

With his Sun, Mercury, and Mars all in Capricorn (and all in the First House of Persona and Personality), Cage is a decidedly sober individual. His Mercury in Capricorn marks him as someone who is practical, logical, and well-thought-out in manner and speech (this is the Planet of Communication, after all). As Mars, the Planet of Passion, is also in Capricorn, expect the actor to be super-ambitious albeit responsible and reliable along the way. With this man, his word is his bond, and he wants others to know he can be

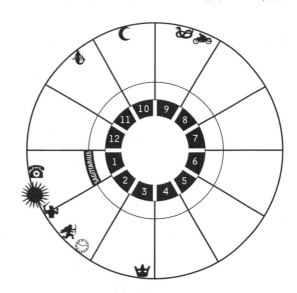

Why is Nicolas Cage driven to succeed?

With his Sun ☀, Mercury ☎, and Mars ⚒ all in Capricorn, Cage is hardworking and super-ambitious. And he's just warming up, since Caps get better with age!

counted on. (It's no surprise that Cage changed his very famous name — he wanted to achieve his successes on his own.)

Thanks to Venus in Aquarius, Cage's amorous side is a real revelation. In affairs of the heart, the actor takes a more radical approach, exhibiting a willingness to try anything once and keeping things both unpredictable and hot. Think of Cage as a wolf in sheep's clothing when it comes to romance! The actor will be rather unconventional when it comes to relationships and will also crave intellectual stimulation from those he holds dear. Finally, he can't fathom a possessive or restrictive relationship.

Looking at Cage's chart more closely, we see his Venus conjunct, or next to, Saturn, the most disciplined of planets. This shows us someone who won't take romance lightly. He is serious and responsible where his mate is concerned and is in it for keeps. Additionally, Neptune, the Planet of Illusion and Make-Believe, is making a square to Venus. This is a challenging placement and would indicate that Cage won't always see his romantic relationship for what it is. He may have a tendency to see what he wants to see and will be upset if the picture differs. Lastly, Cage has a majority of planets in Earth Signs, pegging him as stable, grounded, and not one to trade on instinct; the actor also has most of his planets in Cardinal Signs (Aries, Cancer, Libra, Capricorn), marking him as an initiator and one who gets things done.

Birth time source: Lois Rodden

Jim Carrey

BORN: JANUARY 17, 1962 TORONTO, CANADA

He's a rubber-faced renegade reminiscent of comedian Jerry Lewis. Capricorn Jim Carrey, a master at physical comedy, was a cut-up from early on. Dropping out of high school, he hit the comedy club circuit in his native Toronto and soon took his schtick to L.A. A flair for impersonation opened doors for Carrey, among them those of the late-night talk show circuit. An early break for this funnyman came on the Fox TV show "In Living Color," a comedy revue which poked fun at everything and everyone. The comic's biggest break, however, was the title role of "Ace Venture: Pet Detective." This farce showed that Carrey was a laugh-a-minute man who considered no joke too low. Quick on the heels of Ace were silly flicks like "The Mask" and "Dumb and Dumber." These unlikely successes soon vaulted the comedian into the Twenty Million (as in dollars per movie) Club and led to more mainstream films like "The Truman Show."

Born with his Sun in Capricorn, Carrey is a responsible and hardworking man who seeks perfection from all his efforts. Rest assured that those jokes aren't happenstance! Capricorn's glow is all about success in business and the respect of one's peers. If this leads to money, even better. While ego has a tendency to get in Carrey's way, the comic has a more or less measured outlook on things and knows what he wants.

Carrey's Sun sits in the middle of a stellium, a confluence of three or more planets. In this case, it's a Capricorn/Aquarius stellium made up of Mars, Venus, the Sun, Saturn, Jupiter, and Mercury. The main thrust of this stellium is an intensification of both Capricorn and Aquarian energies. It's worth noting that since Capricorn and Aquarius dominate this chart, things are not well-balanced in Carrey's heavenly plan.

When the Goat and the Water Bearer come together, the result is a very hard worker and one who will find his own niche. (Carrey is keen on owning physical comedy.) This stellium also pegs the comic as someone who must be his own boss. With both Capricorn and Aquarius ruled by domineering Saturn (it should be noted that Uranus is the modern-day ruler of Aquarius while Saturn is its ancient ruler), discipline and hard work are further emphasized for this funnyman, to the point where Carrey may be hard-pressed to see anything other than his work. An overarching need to succeed is also in ample evidence in this configuration.

The presence of Mars and Venus in Capricorn signals Carrey's will to overcome his humble beginnings. With Mercury, Jupiter, and Saturn all in Aquarius, look for Carrey to get ahead by being unique. Breaking down this stellium, one sees Uranus at the 29th degree of Leo and quincunx (a 150-degree aspect) to the Sun and Saturn. This aspect falls right in the middle of the stellium and causes much friction. Uranus's quincunx to the Sun is the mark

Is Jim Carrey as glib as the characters he plays?

Carrey's chart shows a confluence of planets in Capricorn and Aquarius, both of which are influenced by domineering Saturn . The result is a hard-charging man who is hard-pressed to see anything other than his work. It's a Scorpion who will see to it that Carrey doesn't act dumb — or dumber.

of rebellious and willful behavior which may get in the way of Carrey's considerable ambition. It further speaks to a dictatorial streak, abrupt speech, and excitable behavior. With Saturn's quincunx to Uranus, one sees a rebel chomping at the bit. Carrey wants his freedom but also sees the value of discipline. Shall the two ever meet? Maybe, maybe not. The fact that Uranus is at the 29th degree speaks to lessons to be learned by the comedian.

Neptune is square to both Mercury and Jupiter in Carrey's stellium. Mercury's square to Neptune is a sign of illogical thinking. Carrey may be bewildered by his ideas and will struggle to get to the heart of things. Jupiter's square to Neptune doesn't fare much better: Carrey's judgment may be impaired, and he will be misled easily. The comic is fair game for manipulators, although others may find him to be so out there that they'll just leave him alone. Lastly, Jupiter and Saturn finds themselves quincunx Pluto in this stellium. Jupiter's quincunx to Pluto highlights a disregard for principles and disrespect of the law while Saturn's quincunx to Pluto speaks to greed and ruthless ambition. Bottom line: the Plutonian energy here is all about power and turning that power into money — whatever the price.

A quick peek at Carrey's Moon in Gemini marks the comedian as restless yet fluid. The comic can do two things at once and do them both well; knowing a little about a lot is also in the mix. Interestingly enough, while Carrey is good at making people laugh, he can flip to his dark side in no time flat.

Birth time source: not available. As a result, references to the Rising Sign, Moon, and Houses may be omitted from this profile.

Mel Gibson

BORN: JANUARY 3, 1956 4:45 PM PEEKSKILL, NEW YORK USA

New York kid as Aussie bloke? That's exactly what happened to Capricorn Mel Gibson. The family Gibson moved Down Under while Mel was still a kid, prompting him to trade East Coast barbs for the occasional barroom brawl. Gibson studied drama in his new homeland and got his first break when he was cast as the Australian he-man in the film "Mad Max." The actor followed this up with the more subdued "Gallipoli" and the intrigue-filled "The Year of Living Dangerously" opposite Sigourney Weaver. Marvelous Mel found his niche, however, as the fast-talking, faster-acting detective in "Lethal Weapon," a film which has become a franchise. Shifting into action of the historical kind, Gibson took the direc- tor's chair (he also acted and produced) for "Braveheart" and proceeded to nab two Oscars. Returning to action as we know it, the man with the blazing blue eyes starred in "Ransom" and "Conspiracy Theory" and never looked better.

Born with his Sun in Capricorn, Gibson is ambitious to the max. The actor is business-like and methodical in his quest for success. Those graced by the Goat are also responsible and traditional folks who don't make waves. That said, crossing Gibson can make him unforgiving; he's also likely to (discreetly) seek the limelight. The best news, however, is that Gibson, like most Caps, is likely to get better the older he gets. Yes, better. With his Sun in the Sixth House of Detail, Gibson could drive you nuts with his nitpickiness. The man is almost militant in his zeal (for detail) and probably runs his family like an Army platoon. It's no surprise that he assembled a cast of thousands for "Braveheart" — Gibson knows how to keep the masses in sync.

Thanks to his Moon in Libra, the lethal actor must be in a relationship at all times. Mel wants harmony, and that includes some manners from his brood. Libra in the sphere of emotions speaks to one who is sociable, gracious, and tactful. Since the Moon is in the Fourth House here and conjunct the I.C., Mel's Moon is in the most private part of the chart. Consequently, look for Gibson's home to be lovely and his relationships mannered and discreet. Further, the actor doesn't really let others know how he's feeling. With the Moon in its own House in Gibson's chart, look for the actor to value his ancestral roots and to keep his own family out of the spotlight.

It's a Rising Sign of Cancer which marks Mel as a family man. The emotional and sensitive Crab is a great protector, so Papa Gibson will do much to nurture his kids. With Mercury, the Planet of Communication, in Capricorn at the 29th degree, look for Gibson to be well- thought-out and economical with words. The Goat here is a Sign of mental discipline and sound reasoning. With Mercury opposite Uranus, the actor is quick to espouse radical views and is possessed of nervous energy. Look for Gibson to bully with his opinions or say

Why does Mel Gibson manage his brood like an Army platoon?

With his Sun ☀ in Capricorn (and in the Sixth House of Detail), marvelous Mel can't help but crack that whip. Mel's Mars ♆ is in Scorpio to boot — expect the kids (everyone, really) to fall into lockstep.

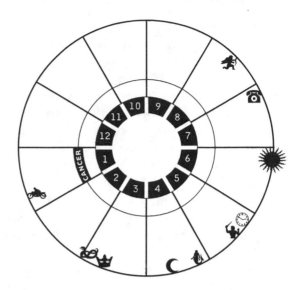

things simply for effect. Since Mercury is also square Neptune, the Planet of Illusion, expect some forgetfulness from Mel and a propensity to believe what he hears. With the opposition of Mercury and Uranus both squared by Neptune underneath, we see the formation of a T-square. Bottom line: Gibson is going to say some strange and unexpected things, perhaps to keep others off balance (he is a private person, after all).

With his Venus in Aquarius, the lover in Mel will try anything once. Lucky Mrs. Gibson! The actor will be unconventional about love and marriage and craves an intellectual match. Since his Venus is unaspected, Gibson may be a bit aloof and disconnected where love is concerned. Mars, the Planet of Passion, finds itself in Scorpio here, a surefire sign of a powerful man. No one will get the better of Gibson, and you can bet he's always got a plan. This lust for power translates, happily, from the boardroom to the bedroom! With Mars conjunct Saturn in Scorpio, look out, world. This tough placement signals physical strength, much hard work, and a love of competition. Since this conjunction squares Pluto and Jupiter, one thing is guaranteed: Gibson does not lose. Don't challenge or cross this man because he will prevail, no matter how long it takes. Lastly, with more Fixed planets than not, Mel may be stubborn, but he gets the job done.

Birth time source: Biography by David Ragan

Denzel Washington

BORN: DECEMBER 28, 1954 12:09 AM MT. VERNON, NEW YORK USA

He's been called the sexiest man alive, but Capricorn Denzel Washington started out in life much more humbly, as a preacher's son. Shaped by his parents' strong work ethic, Washington picked up summer jobs early on and indulged his flair for storytelling in college theater. The actor's big break came via television where he played the handsome resident on NBC's doc-drama "St. Elsewhere." Casting directors soon spotted him, leading to a succession of big-screen roles. Teaming up with director Edward Zwick, Washington turned in a bravura performance in the Civil War epic "Glory" and earned an Oscar in the process. While he drew on his father's oratorical style to prep for his starring role in "Malcolm X," Washington got to have more fun with the pulpit opposite Whitney Houston in "The Preacher's Wife." Married to singer-actress Pauletta Pearson and the father of four, the actor is one busy leading man!

Born with his Sun in Capricorn, Washington is extremely directed toward his goals. The Sign of the Goat signals a patient sort, one who can bide his time while climbing the mountain. These folks are also earthy, self-controlled, and willing to take responsibility. Washington yearns to build something stable and enduring, and to this end he is efficient, organized, and methodical. With his Capricorn Sun, the actor will favor the comforts of a lovely home and will expect to be in charge while he's there. Suffice it to say this is a man who understands the power of money! Further, expect him to get even better the older he gets.

With his Moon in Aquarius, Washington is a man of two worlds. His traditional and conservative Capricornian nature is set on its ear by his wild and rebellious Aquarian Moon. As the Moon is the arbiter of feelings, expect Washington to break the mold where his sentiments are concerned. He will make his own rules with respect to his emotions, and they may be way out there. It's also worth noting that Washington's Moon makes no major aspect to any other planet. The astral picture painted here is of a man who can be disconnected from his emotions, even cold and aloof. The Capricorn presence reinforces this.

Thanks to a Rising Sign of Libra, however, Washington knows how to paint a pretty picture. His appearance to the world will be of one who is charming and sociable and a seeker of harmony. He will also function best when teamed up with another. The actor's Mercury, the Planet of Communication, comes together with his Sun in Capricorn. Thus, we see someone who's thinking is practical, logical, and well-ordered — in other words, smooth. Think of Washington's silky star turn in "Devil in a Blue Dress," as the emphasis in this alignment is one of controlled, studied behavior.

When it comes to affairs of the heart, Washington has his Venus in Scorpio, pegging him as one hot tamale. We may only see the steak, but you can bet there's plenty of sizzle

What's behind Denzel Washington's sex appeal?

Venus ⚔ in Scorpio spells S-E-X. The onetime Sexiest Man Alive will be a hot tamale for a good long while!

underneath! Scorpio energy is all about sex, so expect the Mr. and Mrs. to be having a grand old time — and it's Washington who's setting the pace. While the actor will be very passionate with his mate, he'll also be extremely vindictive if he feels betrayed. A Scorpionic presence in the Second House, the House of Possessions, further signals one who is shrewd with money. Washington's Venus also comes together with Saturn in Scorpio, telling us this glorious guy is plenty serious about love and romance. Once he's made a commitment, that's it. He sees his primary relationship as a long-term proposition and will work hard to make it just that.

Having his Mars in Pisces ensures that Washington understands compassion and intuition. With the considerable Capricorn influence in his chart, however, Washington might not always get this mellow message. This Piscean placement is also a good one for actors, since it enables them to soak up influences and regurgitate them.

A closer look at Washington's chart shows a greater presence of Water planets than any other, marking our "Malcolm" as intuitive and caring. These impulses, however, will be tempered by the Capricorn and Aquarius influences in this chart, which tend toward practicality and an intellectual bent. Lastly, Washington has more planets in Cardinal Signs (Aries, Cancer, Libra, Capricorn) than any other, telling us that he loves to start things but isn't keen on completing them. So what? We'll take good enough where Denzel's concerned!

Birth time source: Lois Rodden

Other famous Capricorns:

Kirstie Alley
David Bowie
Kevin Costner
Faye Dunaway
Robert Duvall
Ralph Fiennes
Cuba Gooding, Jr.
Sir Anthony Hopkins
Diane Keaton
Val Kilmer
Julia Louis-Dreyfus
Marilyn Manson
Julianne Moore
Mary Tyler Moore
Kate Moss
Dolly Parton
Howard Stern
Christy Turlington
Tracey Ullman
Tiger Woods

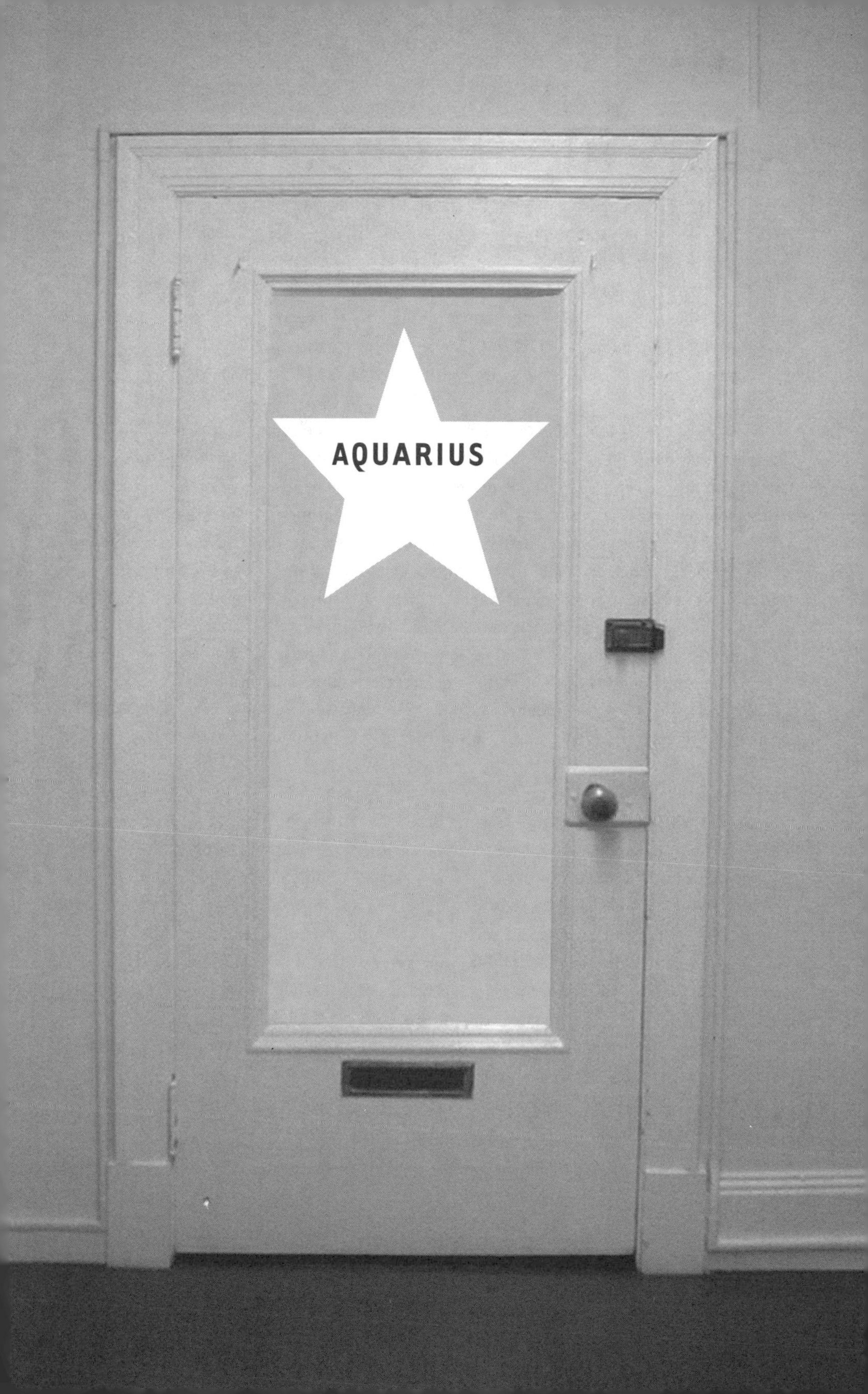
AQUARIUS

Aquarius: The Water Bearer

Since this is the dawning of the Age of Aquarius, how would you feel if you were an Aquarian? Pressured, for one. The next millennium is Aquarian-themed, so others will be taking their cue from you: are you new-agey? radical? rebellious? smart? Actually, many Aquarians border on genius, so they'll probably outsmart the rest of us. That said, those born under this Sign would much rather spend their time creating change for the betterment of all. Aquarians are humanitarians and philanthropists at heart and enjoy putting their considerable smarts to good use on causes of social import. They also enjoy doing this type of work in a group.

Aquarius rules the Eleventh House, the House of Friends. The sociable nature of these folks ensures that Aquarians will have lots of friends and even more acquaintances. It's a paradox of sorts, however, as Aquarians are also fiercely independent and love their freedom. Expect an Aquarian to leave a dinner party midway through if the urge to go surfing strikes. Or to jet off to Rome. With their restless minds and inquisitive natures, there's always something better to do. As this Sign's symbol, the Water Bearer, would indicate, Aquarians are a fountain of ideas, eagerly spurting forth new theories in the hopes that others will agree. If others choose to see things differently, well, that might not be such a good idea since Aquarians can be rather impatient with naysayers. "Sheesh, and I've spent all this time thinking about this, and I'm smarter than they are, and I know I'm right." Ah yes, Aquarians can be a bit stubborn about their stuff, which is in keeping with the Fixed nature of this Sign. They're not doing all of that thinking for nothing.

Aquarius is ruled by two planets, Saturn and Uranus. As represented in Roman mythology, Saturn was the father of many gods while Uranus was the oldest god. Sounds like a stern combination. Anyone disagreeing with an Aquarian may have to face their wrath thanks to Saturn's energy. Uranus, however, instills a more visionary nature. Aquarians love anything newfangled, whether it's the latest high-tech gadget or a bold new plan for feeding the masses. If it's rad as opposed to fad, the Aquarian is all over it. The beauty of the Water Bearer is that this is an individual who is happy to toil in relative obscurity. They're not out to save the world for the glory that such a feat might bestow upon them. These folks are unpretentious yet persevering, happy to sit in their small, crowded offices figuring out solutions to pressing issues. Their penchant for original thought can turn out some doozies, but hey, if it works, so what?

Aquarians border on:
1. Genius
2. Insanity
3. All of the above

The Element associated with Aquarius is Air and with that comes an intellectual bent. Aquarians are among the thinkers of the Zodiac, and they love sharing their ideas and vision with others. Some may find their ideas altogether unique (they are) and even unrealistic (don't bet on it), but you wouldn't want to say this to the Water Bearer directly. These folks can chafe at criticism, and although they can hear it, they'll still believe that they're right. Call it the curse of the smart. Aquarians aren't past putting some of their wilder theories to the test, either, as these folks will try anything once. Many of their best ideas are along the lines of helping the disenfranchised, although they are also inventors capable of creating the next-generation of computers. With the Aquarian's mental might, these folks just might do both.

Aquarians aren't always as they appear, which is just fine with them. They're not overly concerned with what they wear or how their hair looks. Some might even wear a peace symbol around their neck, a nod to the free-thinking, freedom-loving sixties which seemed to represent them best. Those born under this Sign often have a deliciously dry wit, something which can make them attractive to the opposite sex. Leave it to an Aquarian to court their intended in verse, rhyming every passionate plea with the hope of getting to "yes." And you can bet they'll be faithful to the object of their affections.

Sports are important to Aquarians as this is a good way to release some of their considerable energy. Team sports are preferred, since they include the company of others. As Aquarius rules the calves and ankles, the Water Bearer is advised not to make any sudden moves which could cause a sprain. The Aquarian's team is likely to be outfitted in turquoise, aqua, and silver, colors which represent the water they bear.

The Aquarius-born are visionaries with the smarts and heart to make the world a better place. They are freedom-loving individualists with a keen interest in the human condition. They may not look, or act, like the rest of us, but they're great to have around!

Jennifer Aniston
BORN: FEBRUARY 11, 1969 SHERMAN OAKS, CALIFORNIA USA

It's not every actress who is better known for her hair than her flair. Farrah Fawcett, an Aquarian, is one. So is Aquarian, Jennifer Aniston, who created a style sensation with the "Rachel," the shaggy do sported by her character on the hit TV sitcom "Friends." Born into a showbiz family, Aniston studied acting in New York City, where she dabbled in theater before heading West. Hollywood wasn't much of a chore, since the young actress soon landed a role among the company of "Friends." This show follows the ups and downs of six pals in the Big Apple and has been the start to a movie career for most of its stars. Aniston may well be leading the pack: appearing in Edward Burns's "She's The One," the actress has made the most of those TV hiatuses, also filming "Picture Perfect" and "The Object of My Affection" between breaks. Pretty as a picture herself, Aniston is often seen in the company of Hollywood's handsomest men (can you say Brad Pitt?).

Born with her Sun in Aquarius, Aniston is independent and an original. (Her very own hairdo fits right in.) Intellectual as well, Aniston, like most Aquarians, is attracted to unique ways of thinking and is quick to promote progressive ideals. A humanitarian, too, the actress can be shy and retiring at times although she will be viewed as radical and rebellious at others. Starting to sound like her TV alter ego? Since her Sun is square Mars, Aniston will feel the passion of Mars crossing swords with the engaging Sun. The result is impulsiveness verging on a hot temper. With her Sun square Neptune as well, Aniston's self-image takes a hit. The actress may find it easier to escape into her dreams than to deal with reality.

It's her Moon in Sagittarius which speaks to Aniston's need for emotional independence. Ties that bind are for someone else, since this lady would rather travel and move about freely. Although optimistic and favoring high ideals, Aniston's life will appear somewhat chaotic, what with her penchant for moving around. She may also tend toward an unconventional household.

Thanks to her Mercury in Aquarius as well, our favorite friend takes a crisp intellectual look at things and fancies an inventive way of thinking. Progressive may be putting it mildly, since Aniston will be quick to espouse advanced concepts which won't be grasped by everyone. The mercurial Planet of Communication is trine Jupiter here, marking the actress as a smart cookie with a knack for philosophical chatter. No space case here: Aniston is broad-minded and possessed of sound judgment. Mercury is also trine Uranus in Aniston's chart, a sign of resourcefulness and one who isn't easily swayed. Look for Aniston's mind to whiz quickly and brilliantly and for the actress to be deliciously glib. With Mercury trine Pluto as well (yes, Mercury is having a ball here), Aniston's shrewd mental faculties allow her to stay one step ahead of the game. Lastly, since Mercury is sextiling Neptune, the actress is intuitive and spiritually attuned.

Why is Jennifer Aniston so impulsive?

With her Aquarius Sun ☀ square potent Mars ♏ , something's got to give. In Aniston's case, it's usually her temper and a need to act. And act she does (Mars in Scorpio also sees to that). It's a meditative Sag, however, which will bring this lady back to her center.

With her Venus in Aries, Aniston is aggressive with a capital "A" when it comes to love. Expect the actress to be passionate in relationships and to form impulsive ties more often than not. Attracted by physical appearance (hence the hunky Mr. Pitt), Aniston will fall head over heels for someone and then proceed to turn the focus back on herself. Yep, there's never a dull moment with gal! Since Venus is opposite Jupiter in Libra here, vanity and self-indulgence are further emphasized. Ms. Aniston may be more superficial than passionate with her lovers, and she'll also spend like mad. With Venus opposite Uranus as well, Aniston will be an inconsistent lover and in and out of relationships. She'll struggle with the question of companionship vs. freedom — then go shopping.

Mars finds itself in Scorpio in Aniston's chart, a mark of dignity and power. This cutie-pie is one tough lady and won't entertain the question of defeat. The Scorpion's visit to the Planet of Passion also speaks to one powerful sex drive! With Mars close by Neptune here, deceit and illusion play into things. Aniston's affairs may be shrouded in secrecy, though her outlet for this hiddenness will be acting and other role play.

Looking at Aniston's chart a bit further, one sees Jupiter in Libra, the mark of a principled individual. Since Jupiter is conjunct Uranus in Libra, look for Aniston to support some radical beliefs and to have her pulse on what people want.

Birth time source: not available. As a result, references to the Rising Sign, Moon, and Houses may be omitted from this profile.

Michael Jordan
BORN: FEBRUARY 17, 1963 10:20 AM BROOKLYN, NEW YORK USA

Is he air or is he heir? His takeoffs from the hardwood make Aquarian Michael Jordan appear light as air, a fitting visual for the heir of the basketball kingdom. No one athlete has turned the tag "sports hero" into "media phenom" like the self-effacing guard of the Chicago Bulls. A star shooting guard at the University of North Carolina, Jordan was on an NCAA Championship-winning team in his freshman year. He followed this up with Olympic gold in 1984 and 1992 and successive NBA Championships with the Bulls from 1991-93. · Small wonder kids want to be like Mike! Although Jordan retired from basketball in late '93 (shortly after his father's murder) and played baseball the following year, he returned to his true arena in 1995 and proceeded to bring three more championships to the Windy City. Whether he's hitting his fadeaway jumper, pitching for Nike, or shooting hoops with Bugs Bunny (in the movie "Space Jam"), Michael Jordan is always ready for prime time.

Born with his Sun in Aquarius, Jordan can't stand to have his freedom restricted, which may be why he's always running upcourt. More than likely, though, it's to satisfy his independent side and to give him the space to think creatively. Taking the role of athlete and turning it into cult hero fits in with this Aquarian's need to be unique. Jordan is also humane, progressive, and plenty smart, and has limited tolerance for trifling details. Those around him should also be aware of his radical streak.

With his Moon in Sagittarius, Jordan's feelings need a lot of room. The Sign of the Archer signals independence and a need to be free, much like Jordan's Aquarius Sun. The hoopster is also a man on the move, as the Archer's influence will compel him to travel the world. The Sag Moon's glow will make for high ideals in this man, but he may also be felled by daring, reckless behavior. Further, it's likely that Jordan's mother has made a big impression on him. Since the athlete's Moon is square Uranus and Pluto (which are conjunct), a sense of rebellion comes to the fore. Expect Jordan to play the game his way and to make his own rules. Uranus and Pluto's powerful energies over his Moon tell us that Jordan must set his own rules in order to feel good.

It's his Rising Sign in Taurus which makes Mike a marketer's dream. His first impression to the world is one of stability and conservatism in keeping with the Bull's bent. The public will perceive M.J. as Mr. Solid, and his word will be worth its weight in gold. The picture here is also one of persistence and stubbornness coupled with a loyalty and earnestness which are reassuring. Jordan's Mercury, the Planet of Communication, is in Aquarius, speaking, quite literally, to the athlete's intellectual look at things. His views will be progressive, unabashedly direct, and even extreme on occasion. With his Mercury opposite Mars, expect Mike to get his ideas across, even if he has to drive the point home!

Why is Michael Jordan a marketer's dream?

With his Mercury ☎ , the Planet of Communication, opposite mighty Mars 🐾 , Mike can slam-dunk his ideas and make his point extremely effectively.

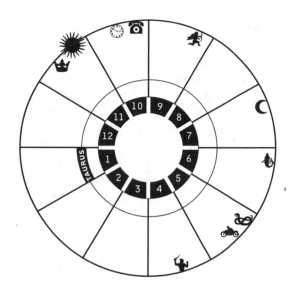

Mars's influence here removes all subtlety and leaves us with one who can be contrary, insolent, and inclined to argue, even resorting to outshouting his opponents to make his case known.

With his Venus in Capricorn, Jordan wants a trophy wife, and his mate Juanita Vanoy certainly fits that image. Jordan will be restrained in the game of love, focusing more on how things look to others. This fits in with Capricorn's emphasis on material, financial, and social status as opposed to raw passion. That said, Mars in Leo in Jordan's celestial plan warms things up a bit, as the Planet of Passion is hearing the Lion's roar. Expect Jordan to be dramatic and outspoken with respect to what he wants. He also needs to be the boss of the game (no surprise here!) and possesses the leadership qualities necessary to propel his team. Although Jordan's demeanor is cooled by his Venus in Capricorn, Mars's lionine energy overpowers it, making it likely that Air Jordan is a tiger in both the bedroom and the boardroom!

A final look at Jordan's chart shows a Grand Cross, or four planets or points, forming a cross in the heavens. Jordan's Cross is made up of his Taurus Ascendant, Saturn in Aquarius, Neptune in Scorpio, and Mars in Leo. This formation creates friction, or the intensity and will to get things done. The fact that the planets in this Cross are all Fixed in nature creates one of the most formidable energies around. Betting against Mike is a bad idea, since he has what it takes to be IT.

Birth time source: Pathfinder: John Woodsmall

John Travolta
BORN: FEBRUARY 18, 1954 2:53 PM ENGLEWOOD, NEW JERSEY USA

Dashing good looks make for many a Hollywood star, but throw a swivel of the hips into the mix and you've got a surefire icon. Aquarian John Travolta, the dream dance partner of women in the seventies, started practicing early. Growing up with thespian sibs in suburban New Jersey (Travolta's Mom was a high school drama teacher), the actor/dancer performed skits for neighborhood kids while studying tap. His big break, however, came off the dance floor: as Vinnie Barbarino on TV's "Welcome Back, Kotter," Travolta shone as the studly oaf. This led to his role in "Saturday Night Fever," the 1977 disco fest which launched a generation's dance craze. Though sexy star turns in "Grease" and "Urban Cowboy" soon followed, Travolta's career nearly ground to a halt by the mid-'80s. Relaunched in 1994's "Pulp Fiction" by director Quentin Tarantino, an older but better Travolta again set screens afire, even taking on the role of President (Clinton?) in "Primary Colors." Actress wife Kelly Preston and son Jett help keep the actor company at home.

Born with his Sun in Aquarius, Travolta is an intellectual man who won't shy away from original ideas. This humanitarian marches to his own drummer and won't be satisfied with the status quo. As is the inclination of Aquarians, he can also be stubborn ("I know this will work!" he'll plead), impatient, and rebellious. Since Travolta's Sun is conjunct (next to) Venus in the Eighth House of Sex, the marquee idol is also the quintessential sex machine. With the Sun speaking to his masculine self and Venus reeking of womanly charm, it's no surprise that women are all over this man. Charm, good looks, and popularity are Travolta's trump cards thanks to this alignment. Since this conjunction is afflicted, however, hedonism, vanity, and laziness may be part of the picture. Travolta will also be motivated by money and darned good with it (hence his numerous houses and a fleet of planes). This lust for money is supported by his Sun's opposition to Pluto, in the Second House of Possessions. Travolta wants to be powerful and yearns for money and power as opposed to the fame they might bring. Lastly, with his Sun square Mars, the actor is nearly unstoppable. The Sun's vitality meets Mars's passion here and the result is an action-oriented man who will not lose.

With his Moon in Virgo, the dancer's emotions are held in check. Virgo's energy yields a quiet demeanor and lends itself to picky, critical behavior. Since the Moon is in the Second House of Possessions and Self-Worth here, physical comfort will equal an emotional Zen state for the actor. With his Moon square Mars, however, things start to rumble a bit. Travolta can become agitated, hostile, and take offense at things (Virgo is quite picky, after all). This alignment also speaks to upsets at home and perhaps as far back as childhood. Since Travolta's Moon is also opposite Venus, rifts with the maternal side come to the fore. The actor may feel separate from his mother or disconnected from women in general.

Why is John Travolta the quintessential sex machine?

With his Sun ☀ pressing next to sexy Venus ♀, the actor can dance (and romance) all night long. Venus's square to Mars ♂ makes Travolta even more attractive to the opposite sex.

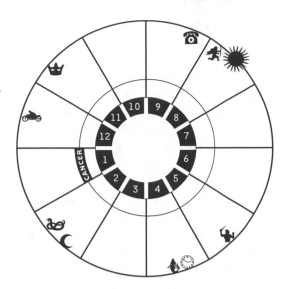

Thanks to a Rising Sign of Cancer, the former "President" is seen as a family man who nurtures his wife and son. He is also seen as appreciating the comforts of domesticity. With his Mercury, the Planet of Communication, in Pisces, however, Travolta may have trouble articulating his message. The actor could come across as wishy-washy, perhaps because he marries his words to his feelings. Since his Mercury is in the Ninth House of Philosophy, Values, and Religion, Scientology is a natural for this spiritual man.

Venus, the Planet of Love, is also keeping company with Pisces in Travolta's celestial plan. As a result, love becomes all-important to the handsome actor, to the point where he may simply be in love with the concept of love. "What's real here?" he might wonder, yet the surreal quality of the Fish won't provide easy answers. With his Venus square Mars, a strong attraction is a given between Travolta and the opposite sex. His relationships, however, may be turbulent due to this alignment, making long-term partnerships a difficult proposition.

Much of Travolta's crusading spirit can be attributed to Mars in Sagittarius. The Archer acts as philosopher and spiritual beacon, giving plentiful strength to the actor's ties to the Church of Scientology. With Mars in the Fifth House of Romance, Travolta's passion also translates to the pursuit of women. The restless Archer is once again on the hunt!

Birth time source: Lois Rodden

Oprah Winfrey

BORN: JANUARY 29, 1954 6:29 PM KOSCIUSKO, MISSISSIPPI USA

The Most Powerful Woman in Television easily transcends the small screen. Aquarian Oprah Winfrey has also added actress, producer, and philanthropist to her resume and shows no signs of stopping there. Now mentioned in the same breath as Hollywood titans Spielberg, Lucas, and Turner, this TV personality is keenly aware of how long her journey has been. Born into poverty in rural Mississippi, Winfrey was bounced between both parents and her devout grandmother by the time she entered college in Tennessee. An attraction to the media and performing led to various radio and TV jobs in and out of college; her big break, however, was the chance to host an AM talk show in the Windy City. By the time she went national with her own gabfest in 1986, Winfrey was well known as an empathetic talk show host who was in sync with her audience. Whether it's her single-working-girl-against-the-world image or her battle with the bulge (or her ongoing engagement with fiancé Stedman Graham), Oprah Winfrey has an everywoman quality.

Born with her Sun in Aquarius, Winfrey is an original and inventive woman with lofty goals. Her idealism might compel her to try to save the world, which explains her philanthropic bent. It also helps to explain her switch to "Change Your Life TV," a very personal attempt to improve the masses. Those graced by Aquarius are progressive and even unconventional in their approach, although they can also be stubborn, inconsistent, and a bit of a rebel.

With her Moon in Sagittarius, the talk show goddess needs her freedom and loves to explore. These explorations tend to lead to the truth, which is where Winfrey's comfort level lives. She is also spiritually inclined, as the Archer is really a philosopher at heart. This placement signals a woman who prefers to learn through experience and is confident in her abilities.

Thanks to her Rising Sign in Leo, Oprah leads with her stage presence. Any insecurities are quickly shoved into the background by the dramatic, larger-than-life Lion. Leo's glow here also speaks to a warm and caring personality and a desire to protect others. Further, the public will see this woman as generous, full of life, and a natural leader. Since Pluto, the Planet of Raw Power, is conjunct Winfrey's Ascendant, the perception of her as all-powerful is magnified. She also has the ability to continually redefine herself, in keeping with Pluto's place as the Planet of Rebirth and Regeneration. The fact that Winfrey's weight had fluctuated, or that the slant of her show continues to morph, are no surprise with Pluto on the horizon. Expect Winfrey to know her own power and to move mountains if need be to get what she wants.

Since Mercury and Venus are both in Aquarius next to her Sun, Winfrey has a stellium in her chart, or a conjunction of three or more planets. The Aquarian influence over Mercury,

What is the key to Oprah Winfrey's success?

Pluto ♇ and Mercury ☎ are in opposition to each other in Winfrey's chart, and both are squaring powerful Mars. 🦂 The resulting T-square gives the talk show host mass appeal and an indomitable will.

the Planet of Communication, translates to one who can communicate in a different way — hence, this lady's singular talk show, one where she is reaching out to her audience in unique ways (think Book Club). When Venus, the Planet of Love, is graced by the Water Bearer, expect someone who is aloof romantically, perhaps because freedom is paramount. Oprah's relationships will be unconventional (that long courtship fits right in) and friendships hold a hallowed space. It should also be noted that an Aquarian stellium is the mark of a humanitarian. Finally, Mercury is opposite Pluto here, giving even more punch to what Winfrey says to the masses.

Mars, the Planet of Passion, finds itself in Scorpio in Winfrey's chart. The upshot is an indomitable spirit with plenty of physical (even sexual) energy. The key to Mars's energy here is the fact that Mercury and Pluto are in opposition to each other and both are squaring mighty Mars. The Mars square Pluto placement makes Winfrey even shrewder than usual and gives her great mass appeal. Mercury's square to Mars means the last word is Oprah's and completes the T-square which is present in Winfrey's chart, a very fixed alignment in this case. Read: no room for negotiation with this lady, not a whit.

Rounding out Winfrey's chart is Uranus, the Planet of Rebellion, visiting Cancer. The result here is an empathetic soul who sets her own emotional guidelines. Lastly, with six Fixed planets, don't expect to sway Oprah's way. This Fixed energy fosters success, since a hint of opportunity coupled with a dose of might are plenty hard to beat!

Birth time source: NCGR

Other famous Aquarians:

Brandy
Christie Brinkley
Garth Brooks
Edward Burns
Sheryl Crow
Geena Davis
Ellen DeGeneres
Laura Dern
Matt Dillon
Placido Domingo
Minnie Driver
Bridget Fonda
Gene Hackman
Paul Newman
Nick Nolte
Christina Ricci
Chris Rock
Rene Russo
Tom Selleck
Skeet Ulrich

PISCES

Pisces: The Fish

Those born under the Sign of Pisces are probably tired of hearing all those Fish-isms: "man, she sure knows how to swim upstream," "gee, he can really go with the flow," and "ooh, she's so fluid" all quickly come to mind. Is something fishy going on here? Nah, it's just that most people haven't really bothered to get to know the Fish. On top of that, these folks are so darn busy living in their dream world that they can be pretty hard to figure out! Those who do try generally wind up all wet.

Pisces rules the Twelfth House, the House of the Unconscious. Think dreams, intuition, and agendas that are hidden. It's not that all Pisceans are hell-bent on being mystical and magical and totally remote. More than likely, this is where their comfort level is, since they tend to be on the emotional side and impressionable to boot. Pisceans are quick to use their intuitive natures to help others. It's as if they have a sixth sense which tells them when another is in pain. As cliché as it may sound, the Fish do indeed go with the flow, letting their radar (sonar?) pick up on trouble spots which they can then fix. This is also in keeping with the Mutable Quality of this Sign.

Ruled by both Jupiter and Neptune, Pisceans have some interesting planets at the helm. Jupiter, the Planet of Luck and Good Fortune, sees to it that the Fish's numbers always come up. Neptune, the Planet of Make-Believe and Illusion, seeks to muddy the waters. Can you say swimming in circles? While Pisceans may be walking around in a dreamy haze, it's not all for naught. These folks are highly spiritual and spend a fair amount of time focusing on the inner self. All of that pondering also lends itself to creative pursuits, so it's not uncommon for those born under this Sign to be excellent actors, writers, and artists. Pisceans feel best, however, when they can put their special talents to good use in the service of others. These folks are sympathetic and compassionate and can't stand to see others in pain. When the Fish can't fix things in a jif, however, they tend to get mopey and even depressed. Lest they flounder, they should seek out the comfort of others at times like this.

The Element associated with Pisces is (you guessed it) Water. This makes our finned friends excellent swimmers, but it also makes them incredibly emotional. These folks could cry you a river if they were down in the dumps. Credit this to the fact that they're so darned sensitive. And caring. Compassionate. Even self-sacrificing. Pisceans soak things up like a sponge, keenly aware of the feelings of others and the dynamics of any given situation. They'd like to arrange for happy endings every time, but when it's not an option, they are prone to procrastination and escapism. Creative as they are, though, they'll generally come up with something which will keep everyone in the pink.

Pisceans are suckers for three things:

1. Dreams
2. Love
3. A dry martini

Put the first two together and you've got the makings of some great fantasies. Dreams for these folks are a great opportunity to escape the sometimes unforgiving nature of the world in which they live. In their dream world, they can create a beautiful panorama filled with happiness and light. Back on terra firma, however, they can become obsessed with recreating their dream state, to the point of playing with mood-altering drugs to reach that exalted level. For this reason, Pisceans should not be given the keys to the medicine cabinet. When it comes to the game of love, Pisceans again have an idealized picture of how things should be. Hearts, flowers, chocolates. Will they ask for more? Doubtful, since Pisceans have a hard time articulating exactly what it is they want from their lover. These folks tend to be shy and quiet and struggle at showing their real selves. They can pick up on what others want, they reason, so why can't others pick up on their feelings? Dream on, little Fish.

When it comes to taking it easy, Pisceans enjoy anything that brings them closer to water. Think swimming, sailing, or a walk along the sea. Exercise serves to alleviate the stresses which the Fish can often feel. Creative outlets such as music and dance are also helpful. When tripping the light fantastic, however, Pisceans need to watch their feet, a sore spot for these budding Nureyevs.

The Pisces-born are compassionate and delight in being of service to others. Their natural sensitivity and creative spirit makes them fun-filled, caring friends. Why swim in a sea of sharks when you can fly high with the Fish?

Drew Barrymore

BORN: FEBRUARY 22, 1975 11:51 AM CULVER CITY, CALIFORNIA USA

E.T.'s kid sister hasn't always lived in an idyllic world. Piscean Drew Barrymore should have been able to leverage that starry surname into Hollywood heaven, but instead, she retreated into substance abuse hell. The child of actor parents and a member of the Barrymore clan (and Steven Spielberg's godchild) started acting as a tot and got her big break at the age of seven when Spielberg cast her opposite sweet E.T. Their precocious kiss should have gotten the actress loads of mileage but did nothing of the kind. Instead, Barrymore proceeded to spend the rest of her adolescence in a drug and alcohol haze, providing fodder for tabloids eager to capture her every slip. After numerous trips in and out of rehab, a more sober actress again took on film roles, such as that in "Scream." Her emancipation as a leading lady, however, came with her role in "The Wedding Singer" opposite funnyman Adam Sandler. Finally, proof positive that this Barrymore also belongs on the silver screen.

Born with her Sun in Pisces, the Sign of the Fish is also the placement of the actor. Liz Taylor and Sharon Stone, to name but two, also share Barrymore's Sun Sign. Those graced by the Fish are sympathetic, emotional individuals who are also intuitive and artistically-inclined. On the flip side of things, Barrymore's Sun marks her as somewhat impractical and prone to escapism. With her Sun at the top of her chart (conjunct the M.C.), the actress is destined for public life. Not only will she achieve success, she is eager to reap the recognition it brings. Although timid at times, Barrymore will generally exhibit the confidence and leadership which are so luminous in the spotlight.

It's her Moon in Cancer which gives Barrymore a wellspring of emotions. The Crab may brood when hurt but can also be intuitive (and a Piscean Sun adds to this). The Cancerian energy here is also familial, so Barrymore will create a nest and enjoys the prospect of nurturing others. Since her Moon is conjunct Saturn, however, a certain gloominess is cast over the actress's emotional proceedings. Saturn's serious energy may compel E.T.'s pal to suppress her emotions, and since it's the Moon's femininity we're dealing with here, much of this emotional damming may be directed toward women. Since this aspect is afflicted, loneliness and melancholy can be the result (think of the Crab in its shell). Lastly, with Barrymore's Moon opposite Mars, impulsive, even angry, emotions may come to the fore. The Saturn and Piscean influences will calm things down a bit, but the bottom line is that this young lady may be angrier than we think.

Thanks to a Rising Sign of Gemini, we see the Drew we all love. The actress's picture to the world is one of flirtatious vitality, a freeform spirit who loves to have fun. That gal in "The Wedding Singer?" That's the one! With the mercurial energy at work here, expect Barrymore to bore easily. Speaking of things Mercury, the actress's Planet of Communication is visiting

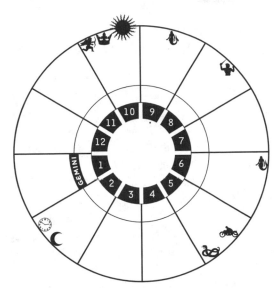

Why was Drew Barrymore such a wild child?

With her brooding Cancer Moon ☾ opposite powerful Mars ♂, combustible emotions are familiar to the actress. Luckily, Barrymore's Pisces Sun ☀ calms things down a bit.

Aquarius in the heavens. As a result, Barrymore is outspoken and possessed of some fairly radical ideas. Her thought process marks her as an individual and a humanist (the latter quality supported by her Pisces Sun). With Mercury living in the Ninth House of Philosophy, Barrymore adores deep and meaningful conversations. She is cutting edge as well (the Queen of Gen X?).

Barrymore's Venus, the Planet of Love, is in Pisces at the 29th degree. Plain and simple, the actress is in love with love. She craves affection and will be tender and sentimental once she's got it. Having this placement at the 29th degree means Barrymore has lessons to learn in the game of love; thanks to the Fish, this romantic views her liaisons through rose-colored glasses. All is not lost, however, since Barrymore has her Venus conjunct Jupiter, the Planet of Luck. The actress will be lucky in love despite herself! She won't restrain herself when socializing and will be the party girl in town. This charmed placement also speaks to one who loves elegance and good living. Lastly, the actress's luck here is with both love and money – a winning combination indeed.

With Mars in Capricorn, Barrymore's Planet of Passion gets a visit from the serious Goat. Think ambition and hard work and one who will succeed despite the odds. Since Mars is in the Eighth House of Sex, success translates to the bedroom as well! Lastly, the six Water planets in her chart peg Barrymore as an exceedingly emotional person. As a result, she'll always find someone wanting to take care of her, about right for E.T.'s kid sis.

Birth time source: Lois Rodden

Sharon Stone

BORN: MARCH 10, 1958 MEADVILLE, PENNSYLVANIA USA

Glamour wasn't part of the plan in small town, blue-collar Meadville, Pennsylvania, which may be why Piscean Sharon Stone developed a plan of her own. This smart cookie (that IQ of 154 is no joke) started her star-struck career as a model and struggled hard to be taken seriously as an actress. Stone's first break was opposite he-man Arnold Schwarzenegger in the futuristic film "Total Recall." The actress parlayed this sliver of fame into the lead in "Basic Instinct," a film which redefined cigarette smoking and showed ladies how not to sit. Reveling in her newfound role as Queen of the Screen, Stone seemed to accomplish more off-screen than on, save for her Oscar-nominated role as Robert De Niro's drugged-up wife in "Casino." Forever in the spotlight (this lady really is a latter day Marlene Dietrich), Stone juggles movie premieres with countless benefits (she's a crusader for AmFAR, the AIDS charity) and marriage to San Francisco newspaperman Phil Bronstein.

Born with her Sun in Pisces, Stone is a charitable and compassionate woman who is unafraid of her emotions. Prone to introspection and the Piscean's dreamy haze, the actress may be unreachable at times. Stone is also quick to subjugate her wishes to the whims of others. In her darker moments, Stone will appear truly blue, although it may simply be a case of being misunderstood. With her Sun square Saturn in Sagittarius, Stone's Sun gets a frigid blast from calculating Saturn. The actress can be cold and aloof (was she really acting in "Basic Instinct?") and will find it difficult to reach out to others. Further dampening things is the fact that her plentiful ambitions will only be realized through hard work.

With her Mercury in Pisces as well, Stone's Planet of Communication is at war with Pisces. Mercury is all about talk and logic while Pisces prefers to trade in feelings. Stone's emotional perception blends well with her keen intellect, but she's also given to distorted, wishy-washy ideas. These conflicting energies make it difficult for the actress to distinguish fact from fiction. Since her Mercury is conjunct, or next to, the Sun, the actress is more than willing to act on her ideas. The bad news, however, is that she is slow to see her weaknesses — and her ego also gets in the way. With Mercury opposite Saturn, Stone may feel insecure about her intellectual capabilities. This alignment also pegs the actress as one who doesn't suffer fools gladly. A more pronounced trait, however, is Stone's almost rehearsed quality. This woman has worked hard at the image of femme fatale and wants it to stick.

Thanks to her Venus in Aquarius, this blonde goddess will try anything once. Her husband may find himself begging for more, however, since this vixen has the ability to switch off those feelings in no time flat. While Aquarius with the Planet of Love signals sociability and one who thrives on intellectual stimulation (hence the brainy Bronstein as spouse number

What are Sharon Stone's basic instincts?

Thanks to her Venus ♒ in Aquarius, the sexy Stone will try anything once! An unconventional relation-ship which frees her spirit is what this lady really craves. Look for a Scorpion to add sizzle and spice to Stone's free-wheeling world.

two), Stone is not your average wife. The actress yearns for an unconventional relationship which offers freedom and is free of restrictions. With her Venus opposite Uranus, the Planet of Rebellion, look for Stone to veer in and out of love. The actress will also gravitate toward those who are different and will wrestle with the question of companionship vs. freedom. Financial reversals are also signaled as a result of this aspect. Both Venus and Uranus are square to Neptune, the Planet of Illusion, in Stone's chart, forming a T-square. Venus's square to Neptune is a harbinger of sexual seduction and forbidden romance. The actress may well be unrealistic in love and blind to the faults of her lover. Uranus's square to Neptune looks even worse: chaos is the order of the day. Perhaps Stone should hide under the covers (alone) when she senses impending doom or feels an inability to cope.

Stone's Mars in Capricorn does nothing to soften the image of the actress as ambitious minx. The Goat is happy to work its way to the top and that's exactly what La Stone will do, master plan firmly in hand. That the actress seeks prestige and the respect of her peers is also part of the mix (or is that minx?).

Looking at Stone's chart a bit further, one sees Jupiter in Scorpio, a surefire sign that the actress knows what she wants and believes she can get it. Lastly, with Saturn in Sagittarius, this basically instinctive girl is pegged as a traditionalist who won't hesitate to moralize on the question of responsibility.

Birth time source: not available. As a result, references to the Rising Sign, Moon, and Houses may be omitted from this profile.

Elizabeth Taylor

BORN: FEBRUARY 27, 1932 2:15 AM LONDON, ENGLAND

Few people have captured the imagination of the moviegoing public like Piscean Elizabeth Taylor. The violet-eyed actress started her career early, as the sweetheart of "National Velvet." While many good performances followed (her roles in "Who's Afraid of Virginia Woolf?" and "Butterfield 8" were both Oscar-winners), Taylor's increasingly exciting personal life, coupled with her dazzling good looks, led the media and public's focus elsewhere. Eight marriages, including two tempestuous stints with actor Richard Burton, kept tongues a-wagging, while talk of dalliances, substance abuse, and myriad health woes never let the chatter rest. Through it all, this veteran of the silver screen (now silver-haired) has kept her chin up and lived a life of beauty and privilege. Ever sparkling (yes, those jewels don't hurt), Taylor has campaigned tirelessly for AIDS research in recent years. Despite increasingly poor health, she refuses to slow down.

Born with her Sun in Pisces, Taylor is a caring and compassionate individual who won't shy away from charitable efforts. As is the province of Pisceans, she is also intuitive, emotional, and willing to subordinate her own needs in order to care for others. While artistic and full of creative ideas, Taylor can at times procrastinate and is also prone to periods of melancholy and gloom.

With her Moon in Scorpio, the actress's emotional makeup is truly intense. She will feel very deeply and passionately about things — especially men. It's easy to see why Taylor has had so many husbands: she's forever looking for love, yet may never find the one that fits the bill. This Scorpio energy also gives Taylor great strength of purpose and determination. The flip side here is that the actress can become angry and jealous if things aren't going her way. It's interesting to note that ex-husband Burton had his Sun in Scorpio, matching Taylor's Scorpio Moon and, as a result, bringing out her considerable intensity. Taylor needs to have intensity in her relationships, and Burton certainly delivered.

It's her Rising Sign in Sagittarius which gives Taylor a sense of play. Her image to the world is one of lightness and freedom in keeping with the Archer's whim. It's also got a touch of the exotic with it, and where Taylor's concerned, it's not just the fact that she's a Brit. This Sagittarian Ascendant also marks the actress as straightforward and eager to advocate her noble ideals. With her Mercury in Pisces (and right next to her Sun), however, things get a bit complicated. Mercury speaks to communication while Pisces is busily ruling intuition and feelings. Even though Taylor will give concrete expression to her dreams and make things sound good, she may have trouble recognizing the flaws in her grand plan. Taylor's Mercury is also opposite Neptune, the Planet of Illusion, in the heavens. This cries for a reality check, which the actress won't see. Neptune, the ruler of Taylor's Pisces

Why is Elizabeth Taylor such a hopeless romantic?

Since her Venus 🏃 is cozying up to Uranus 🏍, the Planet of Rebellion, the charming Taylor can't help but hop from one relationship to the next!

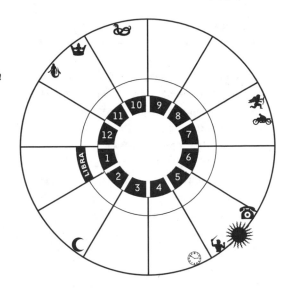

Sun, is afflicted in this case, which tells us that while the actress can indeed perform and take on roles, she may be muddled when it comes to what's real or surreal. Those visited by Neptune, the ruler of "other" realities (dreams, spirituality, substance abuse) have a tendency to live in an otherworldly state.

Taylor's Venus in Aries (and conjunct Uranus at the same degree) quickly brings her back to earthly pursuits. Where love is concerned, this passionate woman will move quickly, be hot-tempered, and exude a fiery sexiness. She's competitive with a capital "C" in the game of love, so don't checkmate her! Threats would only prompt her to move in for the kill (a nod here to Taylor's Scorpio Moon). Since Liz's Venus is also conjunct Uranus, the Planet of Rebellion, she forms relationships compulsively. Couple Venus's yearning for love with Uranus's impatience and Taylor can't help but rush into things. Further, Venus is square Pluto here, speaking to rebirth in relationships. Taylor will end one liaison and begin another without a single hair out of place. Having Mars graced by Pisces does reduce Taylor's stamina and drive somewhat. She'll need to continually keep her spirits up lest she become despondent or even delusional with her world.

Studying Taylor's chart a bit further, one sees Mars in Pisces opposite Neptune. This placement may weaken the actress's physical energy and sap her vitality. Since the Sun is opposite Mars, however, things will eventually get done. Lastly, with five Water planets, this grand dame of the cinema is well-advised to seek an earthier mate.

Birth time source: Lois Rodden

Bruce Willis

BORN: MARCH 19, 1955 6:33 PM IDAR-OBERSTEIN, GERMANY

The big screen might have seemed like a long shot for a small town Jersey kid, but Piscean Bruce Willis had other ideas. Although he acted (and acted out) during his high school years, this man of action had to slog through a lot of odd jobs before getting into the big leagues. Bit parts and casting calls finally landed Willis a plum part: smart-alec gumshoe opposite Cybill Shepherd on TV's "Moonlighting." Unfortunately, moonlighting soon turned to infighting between the series's strong-willed stars, and the successful show folded after a few short years. Willis's consolation prize was marriage to sexy actress Demi Moore and a made-to-order big screen role, that of Detective John McClane in "Die Hard." The pow-zap-bam factor of this film caught on quick and soon spawned versions two and three. Lest he be typecast, Willis stretched himself dramatically in movies such as "Pulp Fiction," "Twelve Monkeys," and "The Fifth Element." Refusing to die, however, can "Die Hard 4" be that far off?

Born with his Sun in Pisces, Willis is a compassionate and sympathetic man with a keen intuition. The Piscean-born are often musical and artistic, which may explain the actor's penchant for playing in blues bands. Emotional as well, Willis has a tendency to be hurt by real or perceived slights and could cry at the drop of a hanky. Yes, our man Bruce is a tender-hearted fellow who loves romance and needs to feel appreciated. With his Sun conjunct the Descendant in the Seventh House of Partnership, Willis marries his ego to his relationship. This man needs a productive marriage to feel whole.

With his Moon in Aquarius, the man from Jersey is a bit detached. Willis will require complete emotional freedom to be happy and may approach his feelings in an unconventional way. Since the Moon is in the Fourth House of Home and Family here, family ties are emphasized. Emotional security for Willis is assured so long as the home fires burn bright. The Moon is also making a wide out-of-sign opposition to Uranus in Willis's chart, signaling a subconscious aversion to ties that bind. While Willis may enjoy the family model, it will be a challenge for him to embrace it fully. Further, with his Moon squaring Neptune, the Planet of Illusion, in Libra, battling Bruce will experience roller-coaster emotions and struggle with his feelings about family and home. The actor may delude himself about his partnership, placing an unnecessary burden on his mate.

Thanks to a Rising Sign of Virgo, Willis does not wilt in the public eye. Rather, the actor will make a nice presentation while appearing modest and dedicated to his work. With Mercury, the Planet of Communication, in Pisces, things don't work quite as nicely. Mercury is focused while Pisces is all over the map. The result is communication which is distorted and unrealistic; Willis will have difficulty gleaning fact from fiction. Since

Why does Bruce Willis need complete emotional freedom to be happy?
This die hard's Aquarius Moon ☽ is making a wide out-of-sign opposition to rebel Uranus 🏍. Ties that bind are out of the question for this free-wheeling man.

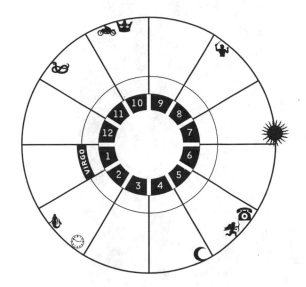

Mercury is opposite Pluto, however, the actor is hep to the game. He sees where others are at and can base his approach around that.

It's Venus in Aquarius which tells us that Willis will try anything once in the name of love. Nontraditional relationships are what will warm Willis's heart, as will a partner who lets him do what he wants. With Venus square Mars, an attraction between the sexes is ever-present, but Willis may not be able to manage it successfully. (When Venus and Mars, the relationship Planets, square off, the resultant friction is challenging.) Willis's Venus is also square Saturn, making for more bad news in the game of love. The actor will have a hard time expressing himself to his lover and may well view his relationship as a business proposition. Going through the motions about sums it up. (Since Mars and Saturn are facing off here as well, a T-square is present in Willis's chart.)

Mars in Taurus adds more practical splash to Mr. Willis. The Bull's meeting with the Planet of Passion speaks to a purposeful man who is staid about money — and sex. The fact that Mars is in the Eighth House of Sex and Finance here further emphasizes this. With Mars opposite Saturn, hasty Mars is met by deliberate Saturn, so it's a standoff. Willis will be uncompromising in both the boardroom and the bedroom. Since Mars also makes a wide square to Pluto, Willis doesn't know how to back down. Ever. With Venus in Aquarius, this completes the formation of a Grand Fixed Cross in Willis's heavenly plan. It marks the actor as extremely stubborn and someone who must get his way. A die hard? Absolutely.

Birth time source: Lois Rodden

Other famous Pisceans:

Michael Caine
Glenn Close
Cindy Crawford
Billy Crystal
Kelsey Grammer
Jennifer Love Hewitt
Ron Howard
Holly Hunter
William Hurt
Jon Bon Jovi
Queen Latifah
Spike Lee
Tea Leoni
Jerry Lewis
Chuck Norris
Shaquille O'Neal
Sidney Poitier
Aidan Quinn
Kurt Russell
Vanessa Williams

Glossary

29th degree See "Anaretic degree."

Afflicted: Used to describe a planet which is unfavorably aspected; squares, oppositions, and quincunxes. An ancient term which is still commonly used.

Air Signs: Gemini, Libra, and Aquarius. Signs belonging to this Element represent the intellectual and thought process.

Anaretic degree: The final degree (29th degree) of any Sign. It is also known as the degree of fate.

Angles: The lines of the chart wheel which lie at 0 degrees (the ascendant), 90 degrees (the I.C.), 180 degrees (the descendant), and 270 degrees (the M.C.). These are major points in a chart and represent Cardinal Qualities.

Aquarian Age: A time period of 2000 years where the influence of Aquarius is prominent. An age lasts for 2000 years and moves backward through the Zodiac. The Age of Aquarius starts at approximately the new millennium.

Arc: An angular measurement between two celestial planets or points.

Ascendant: See "Rising Sign."

Aspects: The angular distance, calculated in specific number of degrees of the chart wheel, between two celestial planets or points. It also provides the nature of the relationship between planets.

Astrology: The study of the influence of celestial bodies on any behavior, activity, or condition on Earth. It is a guide to who we are.

Birth Chart *(also known as a Chart or Chart Wheel)*: A "map" detailing the positioning of the planets in the Signs at the specific moment of an individual's birth. The chart is rendered by using the individual's place, date, and time of birth as the data source for this planetary snapshot.

Cardinal Signs: Aries, Cancer, Libra, and Capricorn. This Quality represents initiative.

Celestial body: A physical form which exists in space, such as a planet.

Composite chart: Two individual charts which are merged to form one. It shows the relationship between the individuals whose charts are combined.

Configuration: An aspect involving three or more planets.

Conjunction: Two or more planets sitting next to each other within an acceptable orb, generally considered within 8 degrees for major aspects. A conjunction gives great strength to the energies of the interacting planets.

Constellation: A group of visible stars in the same section of the sky.

Cusp: The midway point between two Signs of the Zodiac; also used to refer to the start of a House within the chart wheel.

Cycle: A planet's Zodiacal period; the time it takes a planet or point to make one complete revolution in the heavens.

Decanate: The partitioning of each Sign into three equal parts of 10 degrees each. Each part is known as a decanate; every Sign is composed of 30 degrees.

Declination: The arc of measurement in degrees north or south of the celestial equator.

Degree: A degree is 1/360 of a circle. In Astrology, degrees are the commonly-used unit of measurement.

Descendant: The opposite point from the ascendant; the cusp of the Seventh House. It describes one's interaction with another.

Earth Signs: Taurus, Virgo, and Capricorn. Signs belonging to this Element represent a practical nature.

Eighth House: Also known as the House of Sex. It describes shared resources, inheritance, alimony, taxes, and surgery. It is also the House of regeneration, death, and rebirth.

Electional Astrology: The branch of Astrology which deals with selecting the best time to initiate any given activity or project.

Elements: A four-fold division of the Zodiac which is comprised of Fire, Earth, Air, and Water. Signs of the same Element share similar characteristics. Also known as Triplicity.

Eleventh House: Also known as the House of Friends. It describes friendships and acquaintances, as well as hopes and dreams. It rules groups, humanitarianism, and philanthropic attitudes.

Ephemeris: An almanac which lists the Zodiacal positions of the planets and other astronomical data for a given time period. Plural is ephemerides.

Equinox: Means a time of equal day and night. This occurs twice a year and marks the beginning of Spring and Autumn.

Feminine Signs: The Earth and Water Signs, comprised of Taurus, Cancer, Virgo, Scorpio, Capricorn, and Pisces. Indicates passive and receptive energy.

Fifth House: Also known as the House of Pleasure. It describes romance, creativity, children, fun, and speculation. It also rules the dramatic and one's artistic ability.

Fire Signs: Aries, Leo, and agittarius. Signs belonging to this Element represent a fiery nature.

First House: Also known as the House of Self. It describes the outer personality. It is the image we project to the world, our mask.

Fixed Signs: Taurus, Leo, Scorpio, and Aquarius. This Quality represents stubbornness and inflexibility.

Forecast: Plotting the movements of the planets to determine upcoming trends.

Fourth House: Also known as the House of Home. It describes the residence, real estate, ancestry, and the past. It is also speaks to parental influence.

Grand Cross: A configuration in which four planets form mutual squares. It creates much tension.

Grand Trine: When three planets, generally of the same Element, meet each other to form a triangle. The energy of this configuration is harmonious.

Hard Aspect: Aspects which create tension and friction. Squares, oppositions, and quincunxes are all hard aspects.

Horary Astrology: The branch of Astrology devoted to answering specific questions by means of a chart drawn up for the time the question is asked.

Horoscope: In this century, the word "horoscope" has become synonymous with the daily 20-50 word predictions offered in newspapers, magazines, and on the Internet. It literally means the marker of time and is a map of the heavens at the time of one's birth (technically speaking, synonymous with "birth chart").

Houses: The celestial sphere taken as a 360-degree circle divided into twelve sections. These sections are referred to by their numbers, such as "the First House," "the Second House," etc. Houses are generally numbered counterclockwise from the ascendant (starting at the nine o'clock position), with the House which begins at the ascendant known as "the First House." Each House speaks to a particular component of one's life.

I.C.: Immum Coeli. One of the four major angles of a birth chart; this one falls at the bottom of the chart wheel. It is the start of the Fourth House and is one of the most personal points of the chart.

Intercepted Sign or House: A House which appears within another House on the chart wheel. Common to those born in far northern or southern latitudes.

Interpretation: See "Report."

Jupiter: Represents luck, philosophy, religion, higher learning, ethical values, expansion, abundance, and excesses. It also rules long distance travel, aspirations, and judgment.

Lights: An ancient term used for the Sun and the Moon.

M.C.: Medium Coeli. One of the four major angles of a birth chart, this one is at the top of the chart wheel. It is the start of the Tenth House, and it addresses public life and reputation.

Mars: Represents action, passion, drive, and determination. It deals with one's sexuality, force, daring, courage, competitive nature, aggression, and assertion.

Masculine Signs: The Fire and Air Signs, comprised of Aries, Gemini, Leo, Libra, Sagittarius, and Aquarius. It represents assertive and self-assured energy.

Mercury: Represents communication, intellect, consciousness, transportation, dexterity, and the mind.

Modes: See "Qualities."

Moon: Represents the Mother and the women in one's life, nurturing, home, emotions, instinct, and memory. It also represents one's emotional response to situations and experiences.

Mundane Astrology: The branch of Astrology which deals with places as opposed to people; world events and universal trends are the focal point.

Mutable Signs: Gemini, Virgo, Sagittarius, and Pisces. This Quality represents a flexible nature.

Natal: Synonymous with "birth." Natal chart and birth chart are terms which can be used interchangeably.

Neptune: Rules music, television, movies, fashion, glamour, dreams, illusion, drugs, the intangible, and the elusive. It also represents abstract thought, alcohol, the universal subconscious, and the oceans of the Earth.

Ninth House: Also known as the House of Philosophy. It represents religion, travel, foreign countries, in-laws, higher education, publishing, import/export, and ethics.

Opposition: When planets are exactly opposite each other in the chart wheel; an arc of 180 degrees. Creates stress. Balance is needed in the presence of an opposition.

Orb: The space on the chart wheel measured in degrees, between planets and points, by which an aspect may vary from exactness and still remain effective.

Out of Bounds: Planets which are outside the usual north or south measurement of the celestial equator within which planets rest.

Out-of-Sign: Also known as a dissociate aspect; addresses the importance of measuring aspects by degree rather than Sign. For example, a conjunction between a planet at 29 degrees Leo and 1 degree Virgo is within a 2 degree orb but not the same Sign. This weakens the aspect.

Planets: As used in Astrology, this refers to the Sun, Moon, Mercury, Venus, Mars, Jupiter, Saturn, Uranus, Neptune, and Pluto. Earth is excluded as it is our point of reference. In general, it is a major body which revolves around a Sun in a periodic orbit.

Pluto: Rules transformation, regeneration, rebirth, destruction, annihilation, power, and elimination. It also represents atomic power, intensity, crime, death, and the underworld.

Profile: *See "Report."*

Progressions: A method of advancing the planets and points of a natal chart to a particular time after birth. Used to illustrate one's evolution.

Qualities: The Signs are classified by their Qualities: Cardinal, Fixed, or Mutable. Also referred to as modalities or quadruplicities.

Quincunx: An arc of 150 degrees. Also known as the inconjunct; this aspect creates a certain uneasiness and a feeling of discomfort and has karmic lessons to teach us. It is a minor aspect.

Reading: *See "Report."*

Report: An interpretation of one's birth chart. Also known as delineation.

Retrograde: When a planet appears to be traveling backwards from our perspective on Earth. The energy of a retrograde planet is less assertive and more internalized.

Rising Sign: Also known as the Ascendant. The degree at which the Zodiac rests over the eastern horizon of the birthplace at the moment of one's birth; commonly refers to the Sign which is peering over the horizon at that very moment. A new Sign rises approximately every two hours. The Rising Sign represents one's persona and image to the world.

Saturn: Represents discipline, responsibility, ambition, restriction, limitation, and delays. It also rules older people, tradition, authority, structure, patience, and wisdom through perseverance and age. It teaches us our lessons in life.

Second House: Also known as the House of Possessions. It describes your material assets, monetary income, and the potential ways it may be earned. It also indicates what you value through-out life.

Secondary Progressions: *See "Progressions."*

Semi-Sextile: An arc of 30 degrees. This aspect creates unease; it is a minor aspect.

Seventh House: Also known as the House of Partnership. It represents marriage, joint partnerships, ventures, and business partnerships. It also rules divorce, legalities, open confrontations, contracts, lawsuits, and negotiations.

Sextile: An arc of 60 degrees; this is a favorable aspect. The planets involved are usually in compatible Elements. A sextile allows the influences of the planets to work in harmony; it brings forth opportunity.

Sign: *See "Sun Sign."*

Sixth House: Also known as the House of Health. It is about your job, routine, daily responsibilities, diet, employees, pets, and physical fitness. It also addresses a fulfillment of duty and the conscious mind.

Solstice: When the Sun reaches its maximum declination. This occurs twice a year, at the beginning of Summer and Winter.

Square: An arc of 90 degrees which is traditionally regarded as unfavorable. It represents the struggle of two forces at cross purposes. A square brings stress and denotes obstacles which can inspire growth through concentrated effort.

Star Sign: *See "Sun Sign."*

Stellium: A meeting of three or more planets or points which usually occurs within one Sign or House and is a focal point of energy.

Sun: Represents the ego, self, willpower, your uniqueness, and your individuality. It is your identity. It also represents the Father and male influences in one's life.

Sun Sign: What people think of as their "Sign" or "Star Sign." It is the position of the Sun in the Zodiac at the moment of one's birth. The Sign placement of the Sun shows an individual's basic character. It is the core of one's potential and uniqueness as an individual.

Synastry: Comparing natal charts to find strengths and weaknesses in the area of compatibility.

T-Square: The configuration formed when two planets in opposition both square the same third planet (and form a "T" in the heavens). This is a challenging focal point for planetary energies.

Tenth House: Also known as the House of Social Status. It represents one's vocation, career, profession, ambition, reputation, authority, prestige, and achievements, and also rules government. It addresses one's parental influences.

Third House: Also known as the House of Communication. It is the way in which we express ourselves and think on an intellectual level. It also represents consciousness, siblings, neighbors, and our local environment as well as early education, mechanical dexterity, and short trips.

Transit: The position and movement of a planet or point on any given day.

Trine: An arc of 120 degrees; the most harmonious aspect. In most cases, it joins planets in congenial Signs of the same Element. These energies combine with ease. The drawback, however, is the lack of challenge — benefits are derived without effort.

Triplicity: See "Elements."

Twelfth House: Also known as the House of the Unconscious. It represents the hidden or unknown, the subconscious mind, the intangible, sleep, dreams, karma, and spiritual debt. It rules solitude, confinement, fears, sorrow, secrets, hidden enemies, non-reality, institutions, and charity.

Uranus: Represents the erratic, the bizarre, and the different. It rules freedom, inventions, originality, computers, technology, science, electricity, revolution, rebellion, and change. Uranus breaks through barriers and tradition.

Venus: Represents love, romance, beauty, culture, the aesthetic, affection, one's social appeal and acceptability, good taste, harmony, and values.

Void of Course: A term describing a planet that does not make a major aspect before changing Signs. It is used primarily with respect to the Moon.

Water Signs: Cancer, Scorpio, and Pisces. Signs belonging to this Element represent an emotional, sensitive, and intuitive nature.

Zodiac: From the Greek "zodiakos," literally meaning "circle of animals." A band in the heavens divided into twelve Signs, each containing 30 degrees of longitude and acting as the barometer for various human traits.

The Authors

Kelli Fox is an accredited Astrologer with the American Federation of Astrologers. A native of Australia, Kelli has studied Astrology in her native land as well as in the UK and the USA. Her lifetime passion for Astrology led to the development of http://astrology.net, the leading astrological resource on the Internet. Kelli's mission for Astrology.net is to bring Astrology to a worldwide audience and to help people use Astrology as a guide for everyday life.

Elaine Sosa is the editor of Astrozine, a celebrity astrological webzine published by Astrology.net. http://www.astrozine.com features chart readings on celebrities and the newsmakers of the day. When not peering into the "stars of the stars," Elaine writes about food and travel for both print and Internet publications. She fancies herself a road sage — guided, of course, by the stars.

Special Offer

If you can't visit us online at http://astrology.net/bookoffer, you can still take advantage of this great offer and receive a discounted, personalized astrological chart. Please complete the information requested below and submit this form along with check or money order (US currency only) for only $12.95 (includes shipping and handling) or enter your credit card number below.

Complete this form:

Your Name:

Your Address:

City   State   Zip Code

Your Phone Number

Your Email Address

Ship To: *check here if same as above_____*

Name:

Address:

City   State   Zip Code

Phone Number

Email Address

Information for Chart

Birth Date: Birth Time:

Birthplace (include City, State, and Country):

This Chart is for:

Make check payable to: Astrology.net   *Mail Form and Payment To:*
Your credit card number: Astrology.net Book Offer
                                                 PO Box 591692
Expiration Date: San Francisco, CA 94159-1692